HIDDEN
SUFFOLK

Gill Elliott

COUNTRYSIDE BOOKS
NEWBURY, BERKSHIRE

COUNTRYSIDE BOOKS
3 Catherine Road
Newbury, Berkshire

To view our complete range of books,
please visit us at
www.countrysidebooks.co.uk

ISBN 1 85306 637 0

For Mum and Sly

Illustrations and map by Julia Greenwood

The front cover photograph taken by Nick Davies
shows the House in the Clouds, from Thorpeness Mere.

The back cover photograph taken by Julia Greenwood
shows the Edward VIII post box at Bawdsey.

Produced through MRM Associates Ltd., Reading
Typeset by Techniset Typesetters, Newton-le-Willows
Printed by J. W. Arrowsmith Ltd., Bristol

INTRODUCTION

A former (and now disgraced!) cabinet minister told me that the only way to be taken seriously in this world is to write a book. It might have taken me around 15 years to act on this advice, but I can't think of a better subject to be making my debut with. Suffolk has delights in every corner and writing this book has given me licence to poke my nose inside some architectural gems, including more churches than I ever imagined I would cross the thresholds of (I just wish more were open daily) and a number of splendid piles under the county's commendable 'Invitation to View' scheme.

I apologise in advance for any hidden delights I have overlooked; if Volume 2 ever makes it, I will try to include them. Which just leaves the 'thank yous' which, unlike winners at award ceremonies, I will keep short. Many thanks to Jane Baxter at Saxmundham Library for her unstinting help; Julia Greenwood for her lovely illustrations; my family for putting up with hearing, endlessly, about 'the book' and nieces Chloe and Katharine for acting as keen observers and not-bad-at-all note takers when they joined me on some of my jaunts. Finally I would like to acknowledge my sizeable debt to my husband Simon whose editorial input, justly critical at times, has made all the difference. I hope you agree.

Gill Elliott
Kelsale, Suffolk

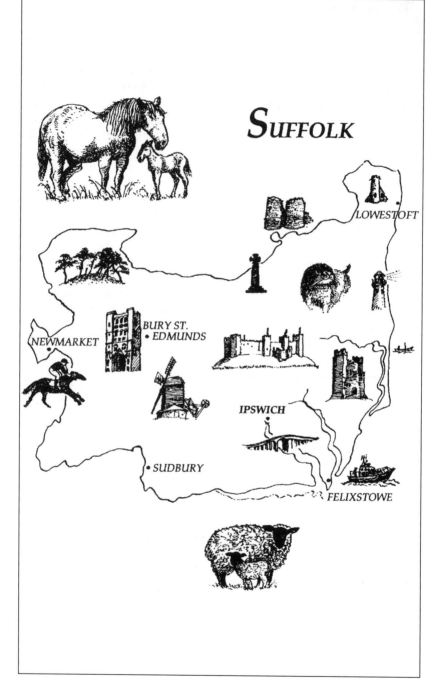

*S*UFFOLK

LOWESTOFT

NEWMARKET

BURY ST.
• EDMUNDS

IPSWICH

• SUDBURY

FELIXSTOWE

ACTON

Miserliness might not be a crime exactly, but it can force people to push the legal limits in a desperate attempt to get their hands on your loot. William Jennens, godson of William of Orange, was so averse to spending money that on his death in 1798 at the grand age of 97, he was dubbed 'the richest commoner in the land'. As he was intestate, so-called relations began crawling out of the woodwork claiming to be the rightful heir to his considerable fortune. The dispute over who should inherit Jennens' dosh lasted 80 years, and was apparently the inspiration for the case of Jarndyce v Jarndyce in Charles Dickens' *Bleak House*.

Some claimants resorted to forging parish registers. But at least they stopped short of murder, which is more than can be said of 17 year old Catherine Foster, who once lived in a terraced cottage next to the village pump where a housing estate now stands. She killed her husband of three weeks, in 1846, by liberally sprinkling his dumplings with arsenic. (Whether it significantly added to the taste, we can only speculate!) Catherine was hanged at Bury before thousands of onlookers; the last woman to meet her fate this way in the town. Her motive, as such, was a desire to return to service.

Perhaps Catherine went to work at Acton Place, the large mansion built by Robert Jennens, father of the Acton Miser and anything but bleak. It was without rival in the area, with a 'Silk Room' and vast stables. It was demolished in 1825 and the only remains – a broken gravestone of Robert Jennens' dog and four plaster busts – can be seen in the church; along with one of the finest military life-size brasses in existence, that of Robert de Bures (c.1302).

Suffolk is rich in brasses, reflecting the wealth created by the wool trade, and the ambitions of its soldiers. De Bures certainly set his sights high, helping Edward I to crush rebellions in Wales for which he received the Manor of Acton by way of reward. By 1331, he held land in fifteen Suffolk villages, including some in Bures from where he took his name. The vicar told me that 20 years ago coachloads of brass-rubbing enthusiasts regularly descended on Acton when this craze was at its height; now there is just a trickle. If you feel the urge to rub the brass, his permission must be sought.

Brass of Sir Robert de Bures at Acton.

ALDEBURGH

—— The queen bee of the honeypots where the sweet smell of the ocean, the sound of the surf crashing onto the shingle and the vision of prettily-painted cottages lining the shore tingles the senses and draws admirers in their droves. So it seems positively churlish to mention the bad times; if it wasn't for the fact that

Marble bust of George Crabbe in Aldeburgh church.

home grown poet George Crabbe penned some of his finest work
on this theme (more from him later). Certainly the Tudor age
brought the good times, not least when the Slaughden port won
the commission to build the *Pelican,* renamed *Golden Hind* for Sir
Francis Drake, England's illustrious sea captain. That's the claim
anyway. Slaughden was certainly thriving with three quays and
a work force of hundreds toiling away, when they weren't
supping ale in the Mariners' Arms; the whalebone pub-sign can
be seen in the Moot Hall museum in Aldeburgh's main street.
There is nothing left of this lost anchorage although one of the
two sailing clubs still bears the Slaughden name.

The tide turned, literally and metaphorically, in 1555 when a
famine descended and the locals had to survive on the sea pea

plant, which still grows in the shingle. (It's a wonder sea pea dishes haven't made their way onto the menus of the achingly trendy restaurants that line the high street today!) The port eventually silted-up and by late Georgian times Aldeburgh was on its last legs. 'So waited I the favouring hour, and fled; Fled from these shores where guilt and famine reign, And cried, Ah! hapless they who still remain; Who still remain to hear the ocean roar.' (George Crabbe)

Until the 1950s, you could take a ferry ride across the river Alde from Slaughden Quay to Sudbourne. You just had to ring the bell and part with one shilling. This stretch of the river may soon disappear if the sea continues to do its worst, but the Martello tower, the most northerly of the 75 fortifications built along this coast, looks like it won't give up the fight easily. Crabbe would have passed it on the way to London on the lugger *Unity*. The poet wasn't exactly flavour of the month with the locals and probably couldn't wait to get away on the early tide. His house was washed away in a storm in 1779, but his bust lives on in the church.

ALDHAM

—— If prizes were ever handed out for the prettiest cluster of hall and church, Aldham would beat the competition hands down. I paid a visit as the autumn sun was setting; showing the flint round tower of the elevated 14th century St Mary's in its very best light. As I turned 180 degrees on my heels, I took in the sweep of the river Gip valley; cows grazing, a dinghy gently swaying on its mooring on the pond. The surrounding green pastures hold traces of buildings long gone; perhaps an earlier settlement wiped out during the plague? My gaze then settled on the delightful hall, built a century after the church.

Aldham Hall has had more owners than occupiers, including the Earls of Oxford and Edward Coke, Chief Justice of England. Robert Clyfford probably owned it once too; Henry VIII's subsidy contributions of 1525 show that he must have been one of the wealthiest men in the area. The hall remained in the hands of tenants and bailiffs until 1911 when it had its first owner-occupier. Some way down the lane from the hall, where the verge widens, is the site of the former village pond and the village stocks. It was near here that I had my first sighting of white peacocks, standing out against the redbrick of Aldham

Gate farmhouse. Close by in The Channel, geese were having a lovely bath in the ford. Altogether a scene too peaceful to be true? Surely not when the Danes were here.

Deans Field (Danes Field), to the north of the church, might well have been the site of a great battle against the Danish invaders. Five bodies with abnormally large bones, possibly those of Danes, were unearthed from what appeared to be a pit, by a local sexton in 1885.

ALPHETON

——— Need proof that Suffolk is a farming county? Come here. An undulating area where colourful cliches drop off the tongue with ease. Fields of golden corn; acres of yellow rape with blood-red poppies occasionally poking through. OK, perhaps only in early summer, but there are other claims to fame in Alpheton, one of the county's smallest villages, dedicated to an Anglo-Saxon lady of note.

'Aelfflaede tun' means Aelfflaede's Farm. Aelfflaede (the suffix is a female proper name) was a member of an influential Saxon family. Her father was Ealdorman Aelfgar of Essex. She was married to Ealdorman Beorhtnoth of Essex, hero of the famous Battle of Maldon fought against the Danes in AD 991. Her sister was step-grandmother to Aethelred the 'Unready' who was to be finally defeated by the Danes under Sweyn Forkbeard and his son Canute, later King of England.

I can say with some confidence that Aelfflaede wouldn't recognise her farm now. The village is split into two by the A134 which was built to give access to the Lavenham Second World War USAAF airfield based nearby, and follows the path of what was once a sheep drovers' road. The old toll house, now in private hands and named 'Tallage', still stands next to the new road. The hall and church lie together in a separate little hamlet that looks as though it is frantically holding onto the past, drawing strength from the few farms which are now worked by machines rather than muscle. The old mill remains too, now a private house.

ASPALL

When I stumbled on this lovely hamlet, with its pretty church and fine Georgian rectory, nothing was stirring. In the former schoolhouse next to the church, a lady was dozing in her chair as I read the plaque on the outside wall: 'Reverend Chevallier, 1865'. A century and a half ago, Aspall might not have had any shops, or craftsmen, but it made an important contribution to the control of larger neighbour, Debenham. The Vicar of Aspall, Charles Hinnery Chevallier, was the sole magistrate in the vicinity and the threat of being hauled in front of the formidable reverend, with his fiery Gallic temperament, was guaranteed to stop a potential felon in his tracks.

Aspall was surely as enchanting then, with the river running for much of its course between copses on its way to the Deben. Behind the moated hall, with its Queen Anne front, is Aspall Wood, the only one of its size in the area (a footpath runs through the middle) which still boasts oaks and several acres of 'ash stools'.

In the grounds of the hall is the Cyder House where in 1728 Clement Chevallier set about making a 'decent' cider, as he could not find any good ones locally. So began the famous cider-making business, now run by the eighth generation of the family in the grounds of the old house. The original granite and timber presses last ran in the early 1970s; as Barry Chevallier Guild explained, they would need a horse to work them which wouldn't go down well with health and safety! He also told me the lady napping was his 98-year-old grandmother who in 2002 will have lived in the village for a third of the time the Chevalliers have – since 1702.

ASSINGTON

At the post office they suggested I paid a visit to the Arger Fen nature reserve and woodland run by SCC. Take the Bures road out of the village, then first left. Unfortunately it was a very wet day and involved my driving through pools of water, up steep slippery hills and sliding down the other side. I made a mental note to try again in the spring, or get myself a 4 x 4.

Access to the hall was not so difficult to negotiate. In 1316 Roger Corbet owned the four manors on which the village was built and turned the monastic church of St Edmund into

Assington Hall. The Coutts family was the first to modify the hall in 1515, and then the Gurdons, who lived here from the end of the 16th century until 1938, when the estate was sold. It burned down in 1957. The Gurdons were enlightened socialists and in the mid 1880s, John Gurdon turned the village into the self-supporting Assington Co-operative. Based on the socialist theories of Robert Owen, the co-operative kept the villagers in work, producing tiles and bricks for the houses which line the Roman road from Colchester. The laudable intention was to 'raise the condition of agricultural labourers without raising them out of their class'. The co-operative was disbanded in 1918, but metal tokens, which were exchanged for goods at the local stores, are still being unearthed.

Numerous monuments and brasses of the Gurdon family can be seen in the Perpendicular style church, site of the Danes' last victorious battle. It was largely rebuilt in the 19th century. The annexe to the hall stands next to the church, and it is hard to distinguish where each begins and ends. I made the mistake of walking to the church via the private front garden to the annexe. I am not alone apparently; the owner told me she regularly re-directs people via the main church entrance.

A secret passage running between Assington Hall and Assington House was apparently used to hide Catholics in Tudor times. The passage comes to the surface in a clump of trees between the two buildings but has since been covered over. Surely worth exploring?

ATHELINGTON

—— I wonder why it was ever called 'the prince's town'? To my knowledge there are no royals among the Atheling family who, as is customary in Suffolk villages, were generous benefactors of the parish church where they recorded their magnanimity for posterity.

The chancel beam of St Peter's has a carving of Edgar Atheling and his wife, and the 15th century bench ends with poppyheads are some of the best to be seen in Suffolk, with designs ranging from small heads to figurines. The mid 14th century decorated flint church took around 50 years to complete as the Black Death hampered progress.

In the Middle Ages, sickness, disease and death were a constant threat. Black rats carried the bubonic plague, which reached England from China via European trade routes in 1348, and literally turned people's bodies black. By the time it abated a year later, one third of the population of England had perished. Labourers, who knew they were in short supply, demanded two or three times their normal wages. In vain the government tried to intervene, issuing the Statute of Labourers; a measure which laid down that wages should be fixed at pre-plague rates. To no avail.

No manpower problems beset the building of the brick and timber 16th century moated Flemings Hall (about two and a half miles south-west of Athelington – just outside Bedingfield). When the snow falls on the stepped gables, it is magical. The hall is a good example of how brick-building skills from Holland have been utilised to compensate for the lack of local building stone. Finding the hall isn't too easy, but once you're in Bedingfield, take the first 'proper' left turn past the post office, left again and then third left through a farmyard. And there it stands among the farm buildings, where you can peep through the majestic gates for a reasonable view of this architectural gem.

🌿 BARHAM

────── If you ever won the lottery what would you spend it on? A splendid hall, on the steep wooded slopes overlooking the river Gipping, complete with Italianate garden, perhaps? Well, thanks to a lottery win in one of the national lotteries which helped fund the Napoleonic Wars, Sir Henry Middleton was able to give his brother William £30,000 to set the foundations for Suffolk's answer to the Villa D'Este at Tivoli. The large grey-brick Shrubland Hall, created, in the main, by Sir Charles Barry in 1852, stands within the village boundary in 300 acres of parkland, and 40 acres of terraced gardens designed by Capability Brown. Peace reigns; or rather it might if the nearby A140 wasn't quite so close.

The Old Hall at Shrublands was the seat of a junior branch of the Bacon family until the 18th century and at the time of the Civil War, its owner, Nathaniel Bacon, together with his brother Francis, were prominent in the Parliamentary cause. Most landowners managed to keep out of the war, helped by the fact that apart from a spat at Lowestoft, no fighting took place in Suffolk. Of those who were actively involved, most supported Parliament, but a significant minority, mainly from large estates in the west of the county, and the coastal Sandlings, sided with the Royalists.

Former Roman roads, now avenues, run through the grounds of Shrubland Hall. There is also evidence of two Roman roads just north of the church, one leading to Coddenham church, the second to Baylham. A coin of Domitian (AD 81-96) was found on the surface of the first. The 13th century church of St Mary was rededicated St Mary and St Peter when the church in Claydon was closed, and a statue of the Madonna and Child, sculpted by Henry Moore, was transferred here in 1975.

In the 18th century, William Kirby had talents in another field. A famous naturalist and an Honorary President of the Entomology Society, the former rector would often sit under a cedar tree studying moths and butterflies, as the village sign suggests. He certainly thought it was peaceful here. A single cedar marks the site of his house.

BARKING

—— Barking might look down on Needham Market, geographically at least, maybe even a little wistfully. There was a time when the village incorporated Needham Market and Darmsden. The metaphorical umbilical cord was cut in 1901. But Barking held on to its Tye – 42 acres of common grazing land. It stands separately from the main part of the village, with a scattering of pillboxes as if to say: 'ancient rights preserved!' The concrete constructions actually have more to do with the searchlight unit stationed here during the Second World War.

An American serving at RAF Wattisham during the war lived in a cottage on the Tye. He used to fly low over the grass, evidently to wave to his wife. One day he pushed his luck and crashed. He lived.

Two of the fine Cedar of Lebanon trees planted in 1720 in the grounds of the rectory by local botanist and rector, the Rev Robert Uvedale, managed to survive the 1987 hurricane. As these fine trees are only supposed to have a life span of around 250 years, they are really on borrowed time anyway. The church, rectory and stables of the old hall (demolished in 1926) stand together sheltered by some further cedars. St Mary's seats 600 and was the mother church to nearby Needham Market. Funeral processions from Needham would travel along the Causeway or 'Corpse Way', as it was called, to Barking churchyard; the bridleway is still open. Chances are the Uvedale family, who held the rectorship for over 100 years, presided at a number of them.

Close to the church are three ancient woods, which are glorious at any time. Priestley Wood, all 39 acres of it, is the same size now as when it was entered in the Bishop of Ely's estate record of 1251. Bonny Wood, at 82 acres, is the largest. Timber from the woods was kept in the fine barn at the edge of the village, for use by the estate. A quantity found its way to London to be incorporated in Gresham's Royal Exchange.

BARNBY & NORTH COVE

—— There's not too much going on now at the old sidings near the Swan pub. But on Christmas Eve 1898, it was crowded. A train had derailed; people were trapped. Along comes Amos Beamish, a huge man of nearly 30 stones, who employs his immense strength to lift the train and release those trapped in the wreckage. He saved lives in the days before emergency services were even thought of and entered the local history books as the Giant of Barnby. The postmistress will tell you about him; Amos was her great-grandfather. The giant is buried in the churchyard where donkeys graze.

A larger-than-life character of the animal variety comes in the form of the infamous dog, Black Shuck, who is said to stalk the roads around Barnby. Looking into the fiery eyes of this hound can result in instant death, so it is said. The name Shuck comes from the Danish 'scucca', a common expression for the Devil or evil spirits. The legend may well have registered with Sir Arthur Conan Doyle during his stay in Norfolk (the other side of the river Waveney) around the time he wrote *The Hound of the Baskervilles*: 'They were the footprints of a gigantic Hound!'

Away from myths and legends, Barnby's hidden jewel is its privately owned broad. Strictly speaking, an old peat digging which has grown over to form an inland lake. It is now a private nature reserve, full of water lilies in the summer and a haven of peace all year round, with pheasants a-plenty. In fact it was part of an old shooting estate. You can't see it from the road as it is shrouded in trees, but drop a line to David Roley at Keeper's Cottage, Barnby Broad, Beccles Road, Barnby and you could be given a guided tour of this unique place.

In the adjoining village of North Cove is the site of the 13th century moated manor, known as Wathe's Hall, next to the early 17th century Wades Hall. Part of the old moat, probably used for storing fish, can be seen on the Barnby Sidings road. The restored wall paintings in the 13th century parish church of St Botolph are worth a look. They are considered by some to be better than the ones in Barnby church.

BARROW

—— In 1780, Mr Macrow of Barrow Hall was collecting tithes when he was shot at (but not hurt) by a highwayman. Maybe the masked assailant rode to Barrow along Shakers Way, a track edged with firs and hawthorn and a favoured haunt of robbers in times past. The horse lost a shoe in the commotion; the highwayman was traced and subsequently hanged on a spot that is now marked by a stone in the pavement, by the village school. The stone is meant to turn over every New Year's Eve at midnight. No one can actually recall seeing this happen, and spotting the stone itself is fairly tricky as it is covered by grass. But I'm assured this is a true tale, although with obvious embellishment. Mr Macrow lived on in the hall – you can see the moat from a footpath at the back of the playing fields – without further, recorded, mishap.

There's quite a large pond in front of the hall. At one time there were over 50 small lakes in the village and ducks and geese are still prominent on the green, with signs dotted around to beware of wildfowl crossing. Fishing is a favoured pastime now, but the ancient craft of hurdle-making (making rustic fences around sheep pens and twisted hazel for thatches) was the preoccupation of villagers for nearly 150 years. The leading lights were the Crack family. Edith Crack had the distinction of being the only female hurdle-maker in these parts. At one time there was a hurdling factory opposite the post office in the main street, but it closed in the 1980s. Curiously, there are no examples of this craft left at Barrow.

The old English word for the village is 'Bearu', meaning grove or wood. Barrow is on the fringe of the old 'Fielding' District which meant it was more open-plan, as opposed to enclosed like most of Central Suffolk had been (an Elizabethan plan is preserved in the Bury Record Office). There are no steam traction engines, as shown on the village sign, clattering through the high street any more. The ivy-clad clock tower, over 50 years old, doesn't make an appearance on the sign though, yet there it stands in the grounds of the old Sally Army hall. The clock is a facade as the original was taken away over a decade ago for repair. Its return is eagerly awaited.

BARSHAM

—— Village signs began springing up in East Anglia in the early years of the last century, when the then Prince of Wales, later Edward VII, commissioned signs for four villages on the Sandringham Estate. Royal events, such as the present Queen's Silver Jubilee, triggered an expansion and the one on the B1062 Bungay-Beccles road must rank as one of the more unusual, with 'stop-you-dead-in-your tracks' appeal. The huge gold petalled 'sun', with colourful flip-side, sitting atop an oak tree trunk, represents the summer solstice and is aligned to suit each pagan anniversary. It is visible across the valley into Norfolk.

Which would please Catherine Suckling, the mother of Norfolk's most famous son Admiral Lord Nelson, who was born in the mainly timber-framed Barsham rectory on 9th May 1725. Catherine's brother, Captain Maurice Suckling, took the twelve-year-old Horatio on his first sea voyage in 1771 and later bequeathed him his sword. The rest, as they say, is history. The house has a priest's hole, a secret cupboard and, according to legend, a friendly ghost which rearranges articles on a dressing table in one of the rooms. Another spirit, a member of the Blennerhassett family from Barsham Hall (built by the Etchingham family in 1348) is said to travel the Bungay to Beccles road with a coach and horses at midnight every Christmas Eve. What it would make of the village sign is anyone's guess!

The grave of a woman reputed to have died in 1584 at the age of 110 years ('Old ladie Ichingham') can be found in the churchyard of the thatched Norman, round towered church of the Holy Trinity. It has a highly decorated east wall with stone and flint flushwork trellis, and a window with around 25 single figures by C.E. Kempe, Suffolk's supremo of the stained glass, who signed his windows with a golden wheatsheaf ('bag of gold'), in the 1870s.

Just near the church, Barsham Old Hall has received plaudits of its own. It was recently awarded a Civic Trust commendation for the restoration work on this fine historic house. It has a young garden feature and a spectacular variety of herbs. It is open on selected days and was once the property of Sir John Suckling, Secretary of State for James I.

BARTON MILLS

—— In the mid 19th century, the Bull Inn played host to the young Queen Victoria on her travels and helped earn it the title: 'The annual resort of the nobility and the gentry in the Sporting Season'. Perhaps the following should be added: 'where good health is restored'.

Let me explain. The Dhoon, opposite the village shop, was the country home of Sir Alexander Fleming from 1921 until 1955, the year of his death. He is said to have discovered penicillin while working in his large wooden studio at the bottom of the garden (although St Mary's Hospital, Paddington, is the official place). One fine day in 1928, by chance he exposed a culture plate of bacteria to the air. Later he noticed that a mould had grown on the plate and had destroyed the bacteria around it. A new era in medicine was born.

The Flemings apparently gave wonderful children's parties on their son's birthday, when Dr Fleming would sport a new bow tie; his sartorial trademark. Olive Jennings remembers consuming the eats in Dr Fleming's studio when it rained: 'And when the Flemings were in London, we had the run of the place which was wonderful as the gardens ran down to the river', she recalls with glee.

The Lark wends its way through the village and was once a busy waterway with a daily passenger service to Norwich. During harsh winters, the river froze and people practised their triple salcos on the ice as they skated to Mildenhall rather than trying to negotiate the snowdrifts on the road.

BAWDSEY

—— In 1886 Sir Cuthbert Quilter from Surrey moved here and set about building his manor on a wonderful clifftop site, apparently blowing up a Martello tower in the process to make way for a sunken garden. He could afford such expense. There are nine turrets at Bawdsey; reputedly one for every million pounds he made.

An Edward VIII post box at Bawdsey.

The manor was bought by the Air Ministry in 1936 and became the base for Sir Robert Watson-Watt's work on radar. Vast metal towers were erected in the north-western area of the grounds, to be replaced by missiles. There are plans to redesignate one of the early Chain Home masts from listed building into Ancient

Monument. A fitting tribute, perhaps, to the work that led to Britain's survival in the Battle of Britain. The manor (now a school) is open occasionally in the summer under the 'Invitation to View' scheme run by the Suffolk Tourist Board and is one of their most popular sites. Even if one lady I spoke to insisted her car stopped working the minute she drove into the grounds. Something to do with radar, she thought!

Perhaps she should have arrived by water. Boatmen have taken passengers back and forth across the narrow entrance to the river Deben for more than 300 years.

In the spring and summer months, up to 300 people a day make use of it. The boat is moored at Felixstowe but can be called over to Bawdsey by waving a white bat, found on the ramp by the river. It's unlikely Edward VIII ever waved across the river to Mrs Wallis Simpson while she was living briefly across the water in Felixstowe. Yet Bawdsey boasts a particularly rare post box with the insignia 'E VIII R' marking what turned out to be the short-lived reign of Edward VIII, who renounced the throne in December 1936, after just 325 days as uncrowned king, to marry Wallis.

BAYLHAM

—— I recommend a walk along the Gipping Valley Path that runs through the village on its way from Stowmarket to Ipswich. Baylham was one of several small communities established on the edge of high ground bordering the Gipping Valley. It pre-dates Stowmarket. The Romans certainly saw its advantages.

Roman roads which run through Barham converge here at the Roman military fort and civilian settlement known as 'Combretovium' (later Coddenham) where a number of Romano-British artefacts from the 1st century have been found. These included a gold statue of the Emperor Nero, which is now in the British Museum.

Baylham House Rare Breeds' Farm, off Mill Lane, incorporates part of the Roman site. It's open between March and October (except Mondays) and offers a chance to commune with rare breeds of cattle, pigs, sheep, goats and poultry. The Roman settlement has not yet been excavated, so there is not a lot to see, but you can get an idea of what life might have been like during the Roman occupation at a display inside the farm.

Baylham House was once the home of Suffolk's arch

bogeyman, the Puritan iconoclast William Dowsing. He didn't spare his local church. The smashed animal heads on the font are testament to that. The structure of the church is essentially 17th century, although it was heavily restored in 1870 with flints picked from the surrounding fields by parishioners, somewhat reluctantly by all accounts. People were recorded as arriving 'tipsy' and 'unable to work'. There are various other examples of flint buildings in Upper Street including the Baylham National School, dated 1860. It is next to the church with sweeping views of the valley. If I had been a pupil there I think I would have spent the whole day gazing out of the window.

BECCLES

────── There is no mistaking the Bell Tower as you approach the town, at nearly 100 feet high. Almost as high as Nelson's column in Trafalgar Square. A structural feat which would not have been lost on Edmund Nelson, Horatio's father, who was curate at the next door church of St Michael from 1745 to 1747. It was here that he married Catherine Suckling on 11th May 1749.

Street names such as Saltgate, Northgate, Smallgate and Hungate hint at when Beccles was fortified. Along Allygate there are a number of attractive properties from different periods, not all as they seem. In the 18th century, Georgian facades were commonly added to older buildings to make them more fashionable. The facade of the Beccles Co-operative Society store, erected in 1895 and further extended in 1912, is largely untouched. Like so many Co-ops built at this time, the building reflects the success of the working class movement founded on the commendable principle of sharing profits with customers.

St Peter's House was certainly in vogue when, in 1760, Dr John Chambers had two rooms, a hallway and minstrels' gallery fashioned in the 'Strawberry Hill Style', so favoured by Horace Walpole (son of first Prime Minister, Sir Robert) in Strawberry Hill, London. The house was extended from its 10th century beginnings as the chapel of St Peter, where fish brought to the banks of the Waveney were blessed, before being sold in the market that stood in front. New Market used to be a large open square. It is now full of shops and the narrow passages between the premises mark the original lines of the stalls.

BENHALL

In Silverlace Green, Kiln Cottage is almost all that is left of the vanished village of Kelton, which used to have a medieval market. The plague was probably to blame for its demise. It must have been taxing delivering letters in this scattered parish. Ayden Close in the Green preserves the memory of Ted Ayden (1897-1971) a much loved, and seemingly multi-skilled, third-generation postman. He could turn his hand to anything, including a spot of hair perming.

His sister was the village schoolmistress. The Duke family bequeathed £1,000 to the village in 1736 for the education of local children nearly 150 years before state education was compulsory. The old school was in Mitford Lane, named after the Reverend Mitford who like a lot of Suffolk clergy seemed to have enough time on his hands to pen the odd poem. Rev E. Holland built the current Dutch-gabled thatched school. Close by is the thatched Delft Cottage with painted geometrical patterns and '1698' on the walls. Mrs Delft was evidently deft with the secateurs and used to keep an exquisite cottage garden, which won admiring comments from villagers as they walked by.

The remains of the garden of the old Benhall Lodge can be seen in woodlands opposite the church, known as The Wilderness. The current lodge, c.1810, with its distinctive Greek Doric columns and parkland, was at one time home to a lord of the manor with a wandering eye. He set his mistress up in a house, the Cupola, opposite the east window of the church from where he would wave to her. I wonder if this had anything to do with a duel carried out in Mitford Lane during Tudor times which involved the Tyrell family, and it is said, a complicated love triangle?

BENTLEY

Speeding along the A12 you could miss this gem lying in a wooded hamlet on the edge of Constable's Dedham Vale. There used to be an underground passage between the nunnery at East Bergholt and the 12th century Augustinian Dodnash Priory (said to have been founded by an ancestor of the Earl of Norfolk) which once stood in Dodnash meadows. All that remains of the priory is a large stone standing in the meadow and legend has it, anyone capable of raising the stone will discover hidden treasure beneath it. Some hope! Dodnash Wood is along a footpath to East Bergholt, past the post office.

The village can also claim to be have been home to one of the few families to have lived continuously in Suffolk since Norman times, the Tollemaches. At the time of the Peasants' Revolt, Richard Tollemache was lord of the manor and reputed to have been one of its ringleaders in the Ipswich area. A century later, John Tollemache moved the principal family seat to Helmingham where he built a new hall, and where the family remains.

At Bentley Hall, the medieval west wing and an outbuilding remain, together with a 16th century hall and 19th century range. In 1668 the Hall was sold to the Gosnold family (see Otley) and in 1974 was perilously close to being demolished. The stunning Long Barn might have endured the same fate, which would have been unforgivable. The timber-framed, 15-bay barn with dark diapering in the redbrick ends, is reputed to be the longest historic barn in Britain.

BILDESTON

—— It doesn't take too much application of the grey matter to deduce that Bildeston was a wealthy wool town in the Middle Ages, famous for producing blankets and blue cloth (and latterly coconut fibre and matting). It has some splendid, half-timbered buildings lining the streets; a testament to the wealth created during this period. The attics of the 16th century Weavers' Cottages in Chapel Street were production centres and the finished products would be dropped through the trap doors in the first-floor rooms. But it is for medical heroism that this village close to Hadleigh is commended.

In the 19th century, diphtheria struck and it was only through the quick actions of a local physician that an epidemic was averted. Dr Grouse spotted an open drain running from the butcher's abattoir, and realising that it was probably polluted, paid for a new covered drain to be built, but not before two of his children had been lost to the disease.

Heroes are not too thin on the ground here. Captain Edward Rotheram fought with Nelson at the Battle of Trafalgar but unlike our great seafaring hero, survived to tell the tale. Inside the church, on the south wall, is a memorial stone with the inscription: 'To the memory of Capt Edwd. Rotheram, RN who commanded the *Royal Sovereign*, the leading ship at the Battle of Trafalgar'.

Near the end of the First World War, the rector threatened to resign the living because of the ropy condition of the rectory. Another parsonage was bought, and the old house sold on condition that the new owner did not call it the old rectory, so it became known as Bentons, after the house where he used to live. It stands in 40 acres of parkland.

I have a feeling Queenie Kray wouldn't have dared to be so fussy. The infamous Kray brothers are reputed to have bought their mother a house behind the post office in the 1960s, when most of the East End's beautiful people paid a visit.

BLUNDESTON

—— What is it about the Suffolk scenery that gets the creative juices flowing among some of our leading writers? Perhaps it is the dramatic sunscapes, always good for a melodramatic dimension to a flagging storyline, or maybe it is the almost unhealthy abundance of churches, some of which are more than impressive and conveniently set in wild, unkempt churchyards full of faded, listing gravestones.

Maybe this is what inspired Charles Dickens when, in 1849, he took a coach ride from Yarmouth to Lowestoft and spotted the sign to Blundeston? With the addition of an 'e' at the end (Dickens apparently liked the sound when he repeated it) the village became the 'birthplace' of arguably his best-known fictional character, David Copperfield. Peggotty and David both attended the Norman church of St Mary and it was from the 'Rookery', thought to be Blundeston House, that David could see the church with its narrow round tower, reputed to be the tallest and thinnest in East Anglia.

'I was born at Blundestone in Suffolk or thereby as they say in Scotland ... there is nothing so green that I know anywhere as the grass in that churchyard; nothing half so shady as its trees; nothing half so quiet as its tombstones.'

The church sun-dial is also mentioned in the story, and it was from the Plough Inn, a coaching inn built in 1701, that Barkis the Carrier urged 'the laziest horse in the world' to take them on their journey to Great Yarmouth. The village's other literary link is with Blundeston Lodge where the poet Thomas Gray (1716-1771) was said to have been inspired to write his famous, *Elegy*

Written in a Country Churchyard, while a guest of his friend, the rector, Norton Nichols. In the 1950s, the Lodge was demolished by the Home Office to make way for a security prison. The school, built in 1726 and still standing, has a story attached. One of the schoolmasters, who died in 1835, asked that his gravestone be topped with three iron spikes to stop village boys from jumping over it; one of the spikes still stands guard today. I wonder if Master Copperfield ever felt tempted by the challenge?

Blundeston church.

——— Tales and legends abound. In August 1577, there was a great storm and members of the church congregation claimed to witness a visit by the Devil. Huge lumps of masonry fell from the tower, killing three people, and an enormous black dog was seen to leap down from the roof. The creature ran out of the great north door leaving the scorched claw marks that can be seen.

Toby's Walks, to the south, takes its name from black drummer Tobias Gill, a member of Sir Robert Rich's Dragoon Regiment, which was stationed in the area to stop smuggling. His bawdy behaviour got him thrown out of a number of local inns, so he took to drinking in nearby Walberswick. One night, in June 1750, returning to camp across the common, he met and allegedly murdered Ann Blakemore. He was tried and hanged in Bury. His body was then left to rot on a gibbet at the murder spot and his ghost is said to haunt the common.

More ghosts are said to stalk the corridors of a glorious ramshackle house, Westwood Lodge, parts of which date back to the 14th century, down the end of a track next to the Walberswick water tower. It is now the base for 'Preservation in Action' and in between selling old Suffolk bricks and terracotta tiles, the owners field endless questions, usually from visiting Americans, about spiritual movements.

Away from things imaginary to things real; Blythburgh is where the Saxon Anna, King of East Anglia, met his death at the hands of Penda, the pagan king of Mercia, in the Battle of Bulcamp in AD 654 on the other side of the Blyth estuary. It is said that his body and that of his son, Firminius, lay in the safe keeping of a church in Blythburgh, but it wasn't the magnificent 15th century Holy Trinity church, the 'Cathedral of the Marshes', standing proud above the tidal Angel Marshes. The church is renowned for its long clerestoried nave roof with angels and original medieval colouring.

It is also the only church I know to have two portaloos, complete with soft loo paper, in the grounds leading down to the marshes. Down the road at the back of the church is what is left of the 12th century Augustinian priory. The ducks gliding on the pond at the wildlife sanctuary opposite, were unexpected delights.

BOTESDALE

—— The steep main street lined with an almost unhealthy abundance of gorgeous Georgian and Victorian houses made me think that if I was looking to film a Dickens' classic, Botesdale would provide the perfect backdrop. Slightly less well-known fellow author, J.C. Jeaffreson, talks about the 'Newmarket' atmosphere, towards the end of Victoria's reign. His account can be absorbed in the Reading Room of the British Library.

Certainly, at one time, there would have been a number of horses here. During the 17th century, when the push for better communications began, travel by horse-drawn carriage, rather than solitary steed, became the preferred option of the wealthy. Carriages needed better roads than horses, and this led to the establishment by the local gentry of the Turnpike Trusts, which levied tolls to pay for the maintenance of the roads. The tariff ranged from threepence for horse or mule, to tenpence for every score of oxen, cows or other 'neat' cattle.

The road through Botesdale was a turnpike from 1769 and taxes were collected at the Round House at the eastern end. As many as eight coaches a day would stop here and some of the large houses, like Crown Hill House, were once coaching inns. Refreshments would be passed from the overhanging upper-storey windows to passengers seated on top of the coaches. The paddocks in Fen Lane would be chock-a-block with horses overnight.

Botesdale was also somewhere to fix yourself up with hired help. The Greyhound is mentioned in the annual Petty Sessions for the 'Hiring and Retaining of servants', which probably resembled a human cattle market. On The Drift, a former drovers' road, cattle reared in the north travelled south on the hoof and were diverted to East Anglia to be fattened before the last 80 miles of their trek to London.

BOXFORD

—— Surely the only village in the country to be known as the spiritual home of British wall of death riding; thanks in total measure to the antics of the late, great showman and eccentric, George 'Tornado' Smith. Tornado was the son of the landlord of the White Hart and during the 1930s, would entertain the locals with his death-defying Wall of Death act in the pub yard. Father would make the introduction: 'My son Tornado will now take the wall', and donning goggles and a black beret, astride a motorbike, Tornado would then ride the wall with Briton, his pet lion, sitting in the side-car. Whether Briton enjoyed his curious life we can only wonder at. But he didn't bolt, and was a common sight walking through the village. He is buried in the pub front garden.

And Tornado's talents didn't rest there. He built an ocean-going boat to sail around the world made from wood taken from a nearby forest. Turning your hand to various skills was not uncommon in Boxford. Skilled trades thrived with the wool trade and in 1622 there were four weavers' Guilds with eleven cloth makers, four dyers, 37 weavers and six shear men.

The old mark stones of this Anglo-Saxon 'ford by a box-tree' can be seen at the iron bridge. The village sign now marks out the territory, graphically illustrating past glories and present strengths. At the unveiling of the sign in 1998, a replica of Tornado's motorcycle and side-car were on display. Dead perhaps, but certainly not forgotten.

BRANDESTON

—— One local churchwarden used to spend five hours 'preambling the parish'. But that was the 18th century and given that lingering is now a luxury, you might prefer to follow the advice of the landlord of the Queen's Head Inn. He reckons on a brisk 40 minutes, starting at All Saints' church, whose former vicar, John Lowes, came to a sticky end.

It is 1645 and England is locked in Civil War. Lowes' paymaster is the squire, and ultimately, King Charles. As far as the villagers are concerned, Cromwell is their man. Added to which the vicar was at odds with his congregation, some of whom considered his sermons to be too long and sometimes mystical. As the elderly priest hobbles down the village street to the church, his black habit trailing on the ground, he can almost feel the villagers' eyes boring into his back, mouthing the words 'Traitor' and then worse still, 'Witch'.

After a bogus trial held at the inn, Lowes is forced to confess to all sorts of bizarre claims by the infamous 'Witchfinder General', Matthew Hopkins, whose dark evil eyes would prompt even the bravest soul to say 'where do I sign?' Lowes was thrown into the muddy depths of Framlingham Castle's ditch and survived, proving he was indeed a witch, before being hanged from the Bury St Edmunds' gallows. He didn't make it back to All Saints' for burial. But the graveyard does boast the tomb of Georgian architect and traveller Nicholas Revett, who co-authored *Antiquities and Ruins of Athens*. The original Brandeston Hall, built by the Revetts and now a prep school, was certainly in ruins after a fire in the mid-1800s. Now the playing fields of the neo-Tudor replacement are a great spot for a grandstand view of budding prop forwards thrashing the living daylights out of each other in the name of rugby, most Saturday afternoons.

Whether Revett ever met his contemporary Margaret Catchpole, is debatable. She used to hide away in Sot's Hole, her Uncle Leader's old cabin, one of many attractive cottages lining the village street. He apparently earned twelve shillings a week labouring; quite a sum in the late 1790s (maybe he was smuggling too?). Margaret came a cropper when she was caught warning her smuggler lover of imminent capture, and deported to Australia. The Reverend Richard Cobbold's novel, *The History of Margaret Catchpole, a Suffolk Girl* (1845), expands on the tale.

BRANDON

A lot has been said about Suffolk's lack of natural building stone, but the abundance of flint makes up for any shortcomings. Knappers Way and Rattlers Road bear witness to this once flourishing industry and there are still a few flint houses which glint wonderfully in the sun; a lasting tribute to good times long gone.

I didn't know flint came in so many colours: black, steely grey, blue, pale violet, brown, honey and white. It evidently has no grain, so can be cut in any direction. Taken from the Dutch word 'knappen' (to crack), flint knapping is known to date from the Mesolithic and Neolithic periods. The flint was used for tools, spear and arrowheads, possibly those held aloft in Queen Boudicca's chariot. Recent excavations have shown that Brandon was once an Iceni island village, accessed by a bridge.

Charles Lennox, Master-General of the Ordnance, brought Brandon to prominence by ordering 100,000 flints for the Tower of London. But Brandon's fortunes really took off when in February 1813, the flintmasters were asked to supply a staggering monthly quota of just over a million musket flints.

A tall order when there were only around a thousand skilled people in the town able to oblige. A French POW captured during the Napoleonic Wars, and put to work in Brandon, brought about improvements in technique and design, such as producing finer flakes using a point headed hammer.

With the invention of the percussion gun the trade declined, although orders were still being shipped out to the Far East as late as the 1930s. There is now renewed interest for gun flints among historical societies, particularly in the States.

BREDFIELD & BOULGE

—— George Crabbe, son of the poet, was Vicar of Bredfield in 1835 and built a new house for himself in his parish at a cost of

Roses around the grave of Edward Fitzgerald in Boulge churchyard.

£1,400; quite a sum in Victorian England. Apparently he found the then parsonage in such a dreadful state of repair he wouldn't set foot inside it. You can get a good view of the new rectory from the rear of the church. It looks in rather good nick.

You used to be able to walk to Boulge church across the fields from St Andrew's church, but not now. The best way is by car. Take the right turn at the ornate, locally forged, wrought iron pump canopy, and then second left past Partridge Farm. Follow the concrete track through thickly-wooded parkland that leads to the gates of the small Norman church of St Michael & All Angels; and the grave of the poet Edward Fitzgerald.

'Fitz' was born at Bredfield Hall in 1809, although he spent most of his life as a recluse, living in a cottage at the bottom of the drive of Boulge Hall. His friends Thackeray and Tennyson occasionally stopped by. Little remains of the cottage or the hall other than the parkland. He is best known for his translation of the *Rubaiyat of Omar Khayyam*, and a rose tree, brought from the grave of Omar Khayyam at Naishapur, was planted by ardent admirers on his grave in October 1893: 'I sometimes think that never blows so red, The rose, as where some buried Caesar bled'.

Fitzgerald was said to have found Boulge dull. He preferred the sea. He once wrote: 'I have always said that being near the sea, and being able to catch a glimpse of it from the tops of the hills and of houses, redeemed Suffolk from dullness.' The church is certainly gloomy, apparently the work (with the obvious suspension of good taste) by brother John. Inside the dark interior hangs a portrait of Edward. Outside by the tower, his plain, stone sarcophagus looked in need of some serious TLC when I visited. There are plans to restore it. Whether the rather bedraggled rose can have new life breathed into it is open to question.

BRIGHTWELL

—— Forget Willy Lott's Cottage and Flatford Mill. *Brightwell Church and Village* is the Constable to wonder at. This tiny picture of oil on wood, painted in 1815, is now at the Tate Gallery, bought for the nation in 1980. We're lucky it came to light. It had been lying low in a London antiques shop for years until someone realised its significance. (Postcards are available in the church.)

It shows a lovely rural scene with the small St John the Baptist church lying on a wooded slope above the sandy valley. Little has really changed in this, one of the smallest villages in Suffolk. The smattering of farms is still there. The former vicarage (now Brightwell House) overlooks the valley on the south side. The church was probably known as Brightwell Chapel in Constable's days because of its close connections with Brightwell Hall, the former home of the Barnardiston family.

Sir Samuel Barnardiston, who rebuilt the hall in 1663, was an MP and Deputy Governor of the East India Company. He became High Sheriff of Suffolk in 1666 and played an important part in the restoration of Charles II to the throne. Samuel's hall was extensive (note picture by church organ) and would have looked very imposing from the present road had the hall not been pulled down in 1753.

A small brick farmhouse, once part of the stables, is all that is left of the great redbrick mansion, as well as the avenue of trees that led to the hall, next to the church. Every spring daffodils grow in a clump indicating where part of the garden used to be. Some wooden panelling from the hall can be seen round the sanctuary walls of Levington church, four miles away.

 ## BROME & OAKLEY

—— No good trying to separate these two villages; they have been joined at the hip, so to speak, for more than 300 years. The houses here formed the original part of Brome Hall estate, built by Sir Thomas Cornwallis, and one of the most magnificent homes in England at the time. And one that might not have seen the light of day. Sir Thomas was accused of selling Calais to the French and imprisoned. But as they spared him his head, when he had done his porridge in 1590, he set about building the hall half a mile east of the church, establishing a new village centre along the way.

Through the generations, the Cornwallis family have served crown and country well: as Household Steward to Queen Mary; Ambassador to Spain under James I and as Governor-General of India under George III. Over the years they have accumulated a knighthood, a baronetcy, a lordship and an earldom. The first Marquis was involved in the surrender of British forces to George Washington at Yorktown, Virginia and his brother Edward founded Nova Scotia in 1748. Not bad going, huh? Americans regularly sign the church visitors' book, no doubt tracing more antecedents who served at nearby Eye airfield.

The Cornwallis family continued to live on the estate until 1823, and there are church memorials to Sir Thomas alongside those to Sir John, knighted for bravery at Morlaux in Bretagne, and Mary Sulyard. They probably lived at Ling Hall, a moated site to the south-east of the church. The Cornwallis cottages opposite the new Brome Hall gates (original hall demolished in 1963) in Brome Street were built in Mary's memory by her father. When the male line died out in 1823, the Kerrison family who appointed the Rev Mapletoft Paterson as rector in 1848 bought Brome Hall.

He lived at the dower house, also built by Cornwallis, at Oakley. In the 1970s it was converted into a country house hotel, now known as the Cornwallis Arms, and is reached via a long avenue of limes. St Nicholas' church, standing among cornfields, is usually locked, but as the floors are sunken, standing to your full height just about allows you to see inside where there is another tomb to Cornwallis, from 1519.

 BRUISYARD

—— Crows resting in the trees are useful tools for transporting you back to when Bruisyard was the seat of the Order of Poor Clares who wore a brown habit, white kerchief and black veil. The Order was founded in 1367 after the chantry college was transferred from Campsea Ashe, in 1354, by the Duke of Clarence and a convent built on the site of what is now the early 17th century red-bricked Bruisyard Hall (left at sign and then on right before church). There is a Catholic shrine on the road outside. After the dissolution of the convent in 1542, it became the property of Sir Nicholas Hare, Master of Requests to Henry VIII and Edward VI.

The stunning Felbrigge Psalter, or Book of Psalms, was probably written and illuminated in northern France, in the 13th century. Once used at the convent, it is one of the nation's treasures now lodged at the British Library. It belonged to Anne Felbrigge, a nun at Bruisyard and daughter of Sir Simon, Standard Bearer to Richard II. Photographs of the Psalter can be seen in a display cabinet in the church.

Leaving Bruisyard for Cransford, a left turn at the Clock House takes you to Cransford Hall, which has survived numerous fires and life as a girls' boarding school and latterly a residential home. Lord Nelson apparently built the original hall for his mistress Emma, Lady Hamilton. I imagine they strolled through the lovely gardens, which spill over with rare species, such as orchids, in the spring.

BUNGAY

—— A good starting point is the tiny museum housed in a little room at the top of the tourist centre. It doesn't seem to be used that much. I had it all to myself and was given the key to unlock the treasures, such as an ostrich egg from Rider Haggard's farm at Bungay and moss from Napoleon's tomb on St Helena.

I also became acquainted with the Bungay song (1856 version): 'Of Beccles and Harleston and fifty more such, With their railways and stations we've heard overmuch; But as for their traffic, 'tis moonshine and boast, Old Bungay laughs at 'em and beats the whole host'. Certainly in the publishing world anyway.

The first Bungay presses rolled in 1795, and since then, as many as 80,000 books have been produced in one week, including the first edition of Lewis Carroll's *Alice in Wonderland*. The mind boggles to think what this coveted tome would fetch in the auction rooms of London or New York today.

What is certain is that the legendary Black Shuck never made it to the Mad Hatter's Tea Party. Legend has it that during an horrific thunderstorm in 1577, the terrifying hound made its way, along with the storm, from Blythburgh to St Mary's church. There are images of the infamous dog everywhere: underneath the village sign, on a weathervane opposite the King's Head pub and on a lamp post near the 17th century Butter Cross. This is a well-known local landmark at the centre of the town surmounted by the figure of Justice; similar to that on the dome of the Old Bailey. It was built in 1689 immediately after the Great Fire, which destroyed most of Bungay.

The town's fortunes took a turn for the better in the late 18th century, when commerce and culture flourished in roughly equal measure. About the time when No 34 Bridge Street (aka The Music House) became a refuge for statesman and author, Chateaubriand, escaping the French Revolution.

BURES ST MARY

—— The serene Stour splits Bures into two. The relevant one for our purposes is Bures St Mary on the river's left bank. (Bures

Hamlet on the right lies in Essex, so keep your passport handy!) The eastbound approach is along a line of poplar trees skirting the river where the moated Smallbridge Hall, built by the Waldegraves in the 1570s, must have impressed the not-easily impressed Elizabeth I who paid a visit or two.

For one of the best overviews of Bures, head (into Essex) under the railway arch, past the old maltings, and as you climb up Lamarsh hill you can linger for a look down the Nene at the church tower and the whole valley as far as Boxted. To the left is the steep woodland above Bevills, a spectacular timber-framed and brick 16th century house. In fields above Bures about a mile to the north-east, is what is thought to be the early settlement of King Edmund, which was built on stilts above the lake and watermeadow. There was a time when Bures was a capital of East Anglia with a number of kings crowned here including, historians believe, Edmund the Martyr, aged 15, on Christmas Day AD 855. Some accounts say Edmund had sailed from Germany, landing at Hunstanton, Norfolk, before travelling to Bures to be crowned. Others say he was born in England and made his way here by other means. Who can really say?

The setting for the coronation was probably the chapel barn of St Stephen. To find the remote thatched chapel you could ask at the stores opposite the church, or follow the Assington road up Cuckoo Hill until you reach farm buildings on your right. Here, proceed through the farmyard, following the public footpath for roughly one half mile. The house next to the barn holds the key to the treasures inside, believed to be the tombs of three of the medieval de Veres, Earls of Oxford. There are also fragments of stained glass in the chapel which in all probability came from Earls Colne Priory. The de Veres rose to fortune on the coat tails of Lavenham's wool trade, which made it the seventh wealthiest town in England.

BURY ST EDMUNDS

—— Under Bury's 'Hidden Gardens' scheme, small ones, big ones, some with trees over 300 years old and even ones created from a car park, can be spied upon from June to September. A good way to see the rural side of this splendid town. Budding naturalists might also search out No Man's Meadows and the Crankles, two adjoining areas between the rivers Lark and Linnet, upstream from the Abbey Gardens.

No Man's Meadows are four low-lying watermeadows separated by ditches, whilst the Crankles is a willow plantation. The grey wagtail can be seen catching insects above the river and sometimes a kestrel swoops down to seize a small mammal. The area was created artificially in medieval times as a result of diverting the course of the river Linnet to provide a millstream for the abbey. The meadows would have been used for grazing livestock, while the Crankles held the abbey aquatics, where fish such as bream, tench and pike might have been bred.

There is still no tower at St Edmundsbury; the only cathedral without one in this country. Now there are plans for a Gothic style edifice made from Barnack stone, which was used in the nave and last quarried over 300 years ago (it has been rediscovered recently in Leicestershire). The layout of modern Bury retains the grid system devised by Abbot Baldwin in which there is a square for God, Angel Hill, and a square for people, Cornhill. On the corner of the Cornhill market place is Moyse's Hall, built c.1180 for a Jewish merchant, and one of the few surviving Norman houses in England.

In the tiny Nutshell pub, a mummified cat hangs from the ceiling over the bar. It probably came from Whiting Street where they used to wall them up in houses to ward off evil spirits. These cats definitely didn't get the cream. They were lucky they didn't get the cheese either. The old Bury cheese market didn't last long, as Suffolk cheese soon got a reputation for being the worst in England. It was extremely hard, apparently.

BUTLEY

——— Fancy some deer spotting? Mary Tudor, sister of Henry VIII, and her husband, Charles Brandon, Duke of Suffolk, are known to have hunted a few even-toed ungulates at Staverton Thicks, in the early 16th century, when they came to stay at the priory. The ancient forest known as Staverton Park is about a mile north of the priory. The oldest part, the Thicks, through which the B1084 passes into Bromeswell, has oak trees up to 400 years old descended from the primeval forest that once covered 80% of the country. A public footpath runs through the woodland where deer shelter among the gnarled old oaks under which Mary used to dine.

Ranulf de Glanville, Justiciar to Henry II and founder of

Leiston Abbey founded the Augustinian Priory in 1171. He was a Suffolk man who accompanied Richard the Lionheart on the Third Crusade to the Holy Land. The priory was once the richest monastery in East Suffolk. Now the buildings are barely traceable among the farm buildings, with the exception of the magnificent gatehouse, which has lavish early 14th century heraldry. Dressed stone, from the river Seine, has been mixed with flint to create a patterned look to the walls, making it the earliest datable building with flushwork decoration.

Another interesting group of trees can be found at Butley Clumps, which according to folklore is the place where monks rested as they carried an abbot to his burial. It is actually an avenue of trees planted in 1790 by the Marquess of Donegal to provide a more beautiful setting for his residence; the aforementioned gatehouse. Originally these were planted in a quincunx, or group of five; four beeches in the corners of a square with a pine in the centre.

The Butley ferry, operating for over 800 years, is a delight of its own. If you call Bryan Rogers, the embodiment of the Butley Creek Ferryman's Guild, before 9.30 am to warn him you're on your way, he will take you across the privately-owned creek from Butley Corner to Orford (for just £2 per adult, £1 per child under ten, and 50p extra for bikes or large dogs). He told me he can also marry you, and sell you liquor, should you feel so inclined (tel: 01394 410096).

CAMPSEA ASHE

—— My introduction to this village was during a party at the Old Rectory to celebrate a family birthday. Not a bad start as it turned out. It was a fine evening and I had a chance to have a look around the glorious hamlet of Ash (one of the two original settlements – the other is Ashe Abbey), centred around the towering St John the Baptist church.

Sadly, the Elizabethan High House, which had stepped gables and ornamental chimneys, bit the dust in 1953, like so many great Suffolk houses. So called because of its four storeys, High House was built by William Glover who was slain in 1641 and whose memorial is in the church. In 1929 James William Lowther, 1st Viscount Ullswater and Speaker in the House of Commons from 1905 to 1921, occupied the house. He painted the original scene copied on the village sign.

In 1195 Matilda of Lancaster, a descendant of Edward Couchback, brother of Edward I, established a nunnery which became a fashionable retreat for women of high birth who were expected to 'take the veil' if they couldn't find a man to marry. St Mary's Priory for Augustinian canonesses was eventually confiscated by the Crown; the chantry college having already been transferred to Bruisyard two centuries earlier. The ruins of the old Ashe Abbey survive in a barn, along with remains of a 14th century timbered hall used to house a small college of canons attached to the nunnery. You can see the remains en route to Wickham Market.

From the church tower, follow the tree-lined path bearing left at a group of houses, go across the pasture, under the underpass, and along the river Deben path. You could well be accompanied by the common blue butterfly, hopping along beside you, in the summer. This route eventually passes the small ancient Oaks Wood, famed for its flora, and leads on to the former Abbey which bloomed for over 30 years until it was dissolved in 1536.

CARLTON COLVILLE

—— You're always conscious of the water close by with Lowestoft on the edge of the village and the Waveney and Oulton Broad defining the northern end of the parish. A former owner of the Bell Inn ran a pony and trap service taking fishermen back to their ships in Lowestoft after a jolly evening in his pub. He probably sent them away with some cured fish as he had a smokehouse at the back of his premises. (As if they needed any more fish, for heaven's sake!)

More community spirit was shown in 1800, when the poor of Carlton were allocated an area of marshland. The annual income of £100 generated from the land is still used for keeping the needy warm during winter. Part of Carlton Marshes is managed by the Suffolk Wildlife Trust (Spratts Water Nature Reserve) and is a haven for wetland birds.

The parish registers were lost when Carlton Hall burned down in 1736. The present house was built on the same site in 1740, with large parkland and grazing horses, and stands opposite St Peter's church, which was substantially rebuilt in the 19th century from the remains of two earlier buildings.

Across the fields from the church in Chapel Road is the late

Victorian Carlton manor house (now a hotel) next to a little gem, the East Anglian Transport Museum. A reconstructed street scene here provides the setting for working trams, trolley buses and a narrow-gauge railway, which visitors can ride on, as well as commercial vehicles like steamrollers. Open during the summer, Sundays and bank holidays.

CATTAWADE & BRANTHAM

—— I challenge you to separate the two; it's impossible. The 18th century Cattawade hump-backed brick bridge with three arches spans the Stour and, along with the railway bridge, connects Suffolk with Essex. During his travels across the Eastern Counties in 1722, Daniel Defoe mentions a wooden one: 'From Harwich therefore having a mind to view the harbour, I sent my horses round by Manningtree where there is a timber bridge over the Stour, called Cataway Bridge, and took a boat up the river Orwell for Ipswich.'

The wooden structure, which replaced a previous 13th century one, was very narrow, in need of constant repair, and you as good as took your life in your hands when you crossed it while a carriage was coming the other way. No wonder Defoe went by river. The bricked version is now a footbridge, replaced by an even newer one to cope with the ever-increasing volume of traffic.

Half a mile from the old crossing is the farm (Braham Hall) where Thomas Tusser, credited with introducing barley to the area, began cultivating in his special way in 1557. His *Hundred Good Points of Husbandry*, first published that year, was followed by *Five Hundred*, offering advice on how to keep a wife. I can't imagine how the two are linked! The farmhouse incorporates part of the 16th century hall said to have been home to Henry Page whose son was alleged to have murdered a young servant girl from Brantham Place. The inquest was held at the Bull Inn. Brantham Place is just down from the church where there is a little known altarpiece by Constable, *Christ Blessing the Children* (1805). Unfortunately it is only a photo; the original is on loan to Emmanuel College, Cambridge.

CHARSFIELD

—— You can just imagine labourers in the fields near Chapel Lane at harvest time, swishing through the corn, their scythes rising and falling in harmony. Until about 50 years ago, harvesting the corn was a lengthy and somewhat chancy operation lasting several weeks, involving most of the community and dictated by the vagaries of the weather.

After the harvest the church would have been decorated with a sheaf of corn and other produce distributed to the sick of the parish after the service. Country people were afraid that if they cut the last swathe of corn they might kill its spirit, so the last few strands were plaited to form a dolly, which was kept and then ceremoniously buried on Plough Monday. The spoils of the harvest was the straw. Bales of straw in the fields the day I visited at the end of summer suggested an enduring arable scene where a pitcher of cider wouldn't have gone amiss. In the mid 19th century the penalties for being drunk in charge of a scythe were quite steep; five shillings, enough when the total earned for a harvest was around six pounds.

The village sign, showing sheafs of wheat and apples, stands outside No 1 Park Lane, the house of Mrs Peggy Cole who played the mother in the film *Akenfield*, based on the book of the same name by Ronald Blythe. It was filmed in and around Charsfield using local people, rather than professional actors. At over 30 years old, this best-selling study of country life is now a classic; recording a farming scene which some of the leading Suffolk families who ruled these parts in the past, might recognise. Like Roger de Bigod who held the manor at Domesday. This farming community on the Deben then passed into the hands of the Tuddenhams, then the Bedingtons, and, in 1613, Sir John Leman, one time Lord Mayor of London, was the bigwig here.

CHATTISHAM

—— The building of the new Wesleyan chapel in 1875 to cater for the surrounding villages of Washbrook, Hintlesham, Raydon and Hadleigh, was to cause some ructions. The new chapel could accommodate 200 people and, apparently, their horses. It caused social division, with the 'lower orders' favouring the chapel, and their 'superiors', the church. Those going to church on Sunday did lose out in some ways. They had to walk there as the coachman could never be called out on the Sabbath.

Farmer Thomas Hayward walked the distance to the church from Chattisham Hall (a white building standing among fields on the way to Hintlesham) which he built in 1864, replacing the earlier Tudor building which burned down. He became treasurer of a forerunner of Neighbourhood Watch, forming local farmers and tenants into groups to keep an eye out for undesirables.

He would have been kept busy in the mid 17th century when witch-hunting was something of a national pastime, spurred on by 'Witchfinder General', Matthew Hopkins. Chattisham's most famous witches were Mary and Nathaniel Bacon who were forced to confess to having sealed a covenant with the Devil, and to have 'suckled' two imps. Most of the victims of witch killings were elderly women, rather past their best physically. As Banquo in *Macbeth* once said: 'You should be women, and yet your beards forbid me to interpret that you are so.' In 1647 Hopkins was put to death when his dubious techniques for gaining confessions were exposed.

I wonder what Hopkins would have made of Margaret of Antioch, referred to in the dedication of the 14th century church of All Saints and St Margaret? She never actually existed as a person, only as a character of pious fiction, popular during the Middle Ages. The story goes she was the daughter of a pagan priest, Aedisius of Antioch, who turned her out when she decided to embrace Christianity. She was imprisoned, and then swallowed by a dragon, but happily not digested by him as her cross irritated his throat and he spat her out. She is depicted on a silver mace at St Margaret's Westminster.

CHELMONDISTON & PIN MILL

—— As Ratty said to Moley on their picnic: 'Believe me my young friend, there is nothing – absolutely nothing – half so much worth doing as simply messing about in boats' (*Wind in the Willows*). I couldn't agree more and this is one of the best locations for those of a similar persuasion. There was a time when the more serious players ruled here. In Chelmondiston (aka 'Chempton') barges and large steam boats that moored in Butterman's Bay transported grain and coal. The heyday for nearby Pin Mill was a century ago when it was the Clapham

Pin Mill.

junction of the East Coast barge trade and hundreds of dockers would spend their working days humping cargo from ship to barge. Only the sight of three decaying old clippers gives some clue as to the village's former trading achievements.

It is now the haunt of sailors on a jolly up the Orwell, or on a serious mission across the North Sea. I have often quenched my thirst in the pub, enjoying the view from the bay window to the hulks heeling in the mud at low tide.

The author of *Swallows and Amazons*, Arthur Ransome, spent many an hour at Alma Cottage, where he wrote *Secret Water*. His fine wooden boat, the *Nancy Blackett*, was kept at the boatyard but now spends some of its time touring the country.

CHELSWORTH

—— Suffolk is a truly lovely county. If you are about to contradict me, come here first. On the road sweeping you in from Monks Eleigh, the sandstone of All Saints jostling for pole position with the deep red of The Grange is a grand curtain-raiser to the treats in store. Julian Tennyson, great grandson of Queen Victoria's Poet Laureate Alfred, Lord Tennyson, thought so too when he paid a visit before the war, when Chelsworth was a village quite unknown.

Perhaps not quite as hidden as it once was, and given that there has been a lot of water under the 18th century double-hump bridge since then, Chelsworth has done well to retain its general gorgeousness. Notably the timber-framed old forge, the Georgian rectory with a stuccoed 18th century front, and pretty reed-topped cottages elegantly lining the long, straight high street.

Park in front of the beamy Peacock Inn and wander over the bridge. Halfway you can lean over the edge and be soothed by the sound of the gentle waterfall, or feel tempted to picnic on the banks of the Brett where weeping willows draping into the river could move you to write poetry of which Tennyson senior could be proud. Cows grazing in fields beyond complete the rural scene, which wouldn't look out of place on Constable's canvas. The horses munching in a nearby meadow could even get Munnings' creative juices flowing.

The terracotta limewashed Grange with divers gables is quintessential Suffolk where houses rely on beautiful proportions, rather than ornamental features. Interestingly, the building looks like a new house made to look old. But here in Chelsworth, there are no fakes.

 ## CHEVINGTON

—— The ancient pathway, the Chevington Way, takes its name from this village which lies halfway between Bury St Edmunds and Newmarket on the edge of the Ickworth Park estate. You can get here via the A143 from Horringer, or on the minor Saxham Road (see Great Saxham). This is traditionally England's corn-growing belt but fields covered with bright yellow oilseed rape, and paddocks with frolicking horses shaping up for Newmarket, have almost dwarfed the cereal fields.

You're likely to see the name of the White family appearing frequently. Four Whites were rectors of Chevington for 150 years between 1776 and 1926. As spiritual leaders and landowners, the family exerted a strong influence; nearly as much as the Lords Bristol of Ickworth. George Edward White, Captain and Adjutant, 3rd Sikh Infantry, fell on 18th November 1902 while gallantly leading the storming party at Gumatti Fort in the Waziri Expedition. Cyril White died in India; John White threw off his mortal coil at Gallipoli, as the church memorials testify. There is also a plaque to Cyril Miles (twelve and a half) who died on 22nd May 1901, from 'the effects of a gun accident' in New Zealand. On a happier note, the Rev John White III's daughter could boast Miss Millais, daughter of the great painter Sir John, as one of her bridesmaids.

The flint house next to the church, and a thatched building with pargeting and chimney atop, stand out from the mainly modern houses on the road to the church. Leaving your car here, the footpath leads to the Ickworth estate. Sir Thomas Kytson, Lord of the Manor of Chevington, built Hengrave Hall around 1538; but would live at his pile in Chevington when he wanted some time off for a spot of hunting in the park. He probably walked back to Hengrave along the Chevington Way.

CLAYDON

────── Claydon chalk used to be taken from the Church Lane pits for processing at the Garnham family's mill in Old Paper Mill Lane (near the village sign). The chalk blocks were lime slacked and later mixed with cow hair to produce mortar and whiting for plastering ceilings. You can still see the gravel pit; a new housing estate grows around it.

Just up the road from the pits is the splendid old rectory (now a business) with possibly the most interesting garden follies you will see anywhere. There are two Gothick towers joined by flint walls, and made up, in all probability, of parts of the old church chancel. There is supposed to be a rather pretty underground grotto there too. (A footpath skirts the grounds.) St Peter's church next door is redundant but you can get a look inside, when it isn't locked. The transepts were the work of diocesan architect Phipson; the south one displayed Henry Moore's *Madonna*, sculpted in the late 1940s, until it was moved to Barham church. The statue was a war memorial, commissioned by Sir Jasper Ridley who is buried in St Peter's.

There is also a brass to Samuel Aylmer who probably built Mockbeggars Hall. The splendid Jacobean, Grade II listed hall (formerly Claydon Old Hall), can be seen across the fields as you drive along the A14. It was built as a hall-house in the 1600s, and was once home to the Bishop of London. Three of its five Dutch gables have gone, along with the 17th century Adam fireplace, but it is still imposing, if not as substantial as it seems. It is only one room deep, rather like a Suffolk farmhouse, and now operates as a grand B&B. As to the name, it could be explained by its size. As it seemed bigger than it actually was, it 'mocked the beggars' who might have hoped to avail themselves of some hearty leftovers in what they assumed would be a magnificent dining-hall. In the best possible ghostly tradition, tales of spirit movements and even human sacrifices, abound.

CODDENHAM

—— I once drove through the high street in a snowstorm. The winding roads were slippery, but the flakes falling over the village made it just about bearable, nay magical. The next time I drove through in warmer climes coming in from Needham Market, over the bridge and straight into what could be described as not just chocolate box, but Hershey big bar territory!

This is definitely the village to walk around. Parking is a problem, with signs displayed by locals in the narrow high street: 'try not to park across our window'. I disposed of my motor in School Road close to Blacksmith's Lane near the Old Forge Cottage. If you stayed in the car, you would also miss out on the nature trail, which you can pick up from the church. Leaflets in the porch direct you first among the many yew trees in the churchyard. But before you head off in search of this genus *Taxus*, take in the glorious view over the deep valley.

The yew has traditionally been planted in churchyards and centuries ago was used for making bows for archers. An archer's family originally owned the house in Coddenham opposite Gudgin's Shop in School Road, and archers practised in a field not too far away. Gryffon House is said to have been the home of an archer knighted by Henry V for his heroic actions at Agincourt. Strange when you think that yew twigs are emblematic of grief.

Across the road from the church are the ancient pastures of Manor Farm, grazed by a herd of Red Poll cows; said to be the only remaining dairy herd of this breed in Suffolk (see Gedding). They looked friendly enough when I trampled through their pastures, eventually coming out by the stile opposite the church. Which is the best exit as it cuts down on the time you have to spend on the fairly treacherous road, with single pavement.

CORTON

—— The waves are now lapping at its heels, but at one time the village of Newton stood between it and the sea. But there are compensations, of a kind. A 20 foot high 'chimney', which had been a deep well, came to light on the shore after a storm.

Apparently with Newton disappearing into the sea, the treacherous Corton Sands were born. These sandbanks, which lie off the coastline, had the first beacon to be lighted by the Corporation of Trinity House in 1609; one of a number alerting Burgh Castle, eight miles away, to any potential coastal invasion. A twenty-three metre flint and rubble building, similar to ones at Burgh, was also discovered here. It was thought to be part of Roman defences added in the 4th century, suggesting Corton was at one time a Roman signal station.

The church of St Bartholomew, although structurally unsound, stands almost majestically among fields of corn a quarter of a mile from the cliff edge. The 90 foot tower has been a landmark for seafarers for the 700 years it has commanded its position. Roman tiles found in the church walls, and ancient coins at the base of the high cliffs, all help to build up a picture of life in Corton when the sentinel was lighting his beacon.

Jeremiah James Colman, of the famous Norwich mustard company, might have marvelled at the view in Victorian times when he had a seaside home, which he built a wall around to try to protect. It didn't help. Jeremiah virtually owned the village, building tenant housing, the hall and a Methodist church. In 1910 the sea was gaining the upper hand and he was forced to move on. Jeremiah was a lover of art and it is largely thanks to him that Norwich has the largest collection of John Sell Cotman (tutor of Dante Gabriel Rossetti) paintings in the world. Suffolk's loss was Norfolk's gain.

COTTON

—— Arguably the most significant house here is Cotton Hall, reputed to have been the meeting place of the Gunpowder Plotters who nearly succeeded in blowing up the Houses of Parliament in 1605. Guy (Guido) Fawkes, an explosives expert serving with the Spanish army, was recruited in Flanders by Thomas Winter, a member of a Roman Catholic group plotting to rid the country of the Protestant King James I and his Parliament.

Fawkes was discovered in the House of Lords' cellar with a burning fuse in his hand, ironically by the Earl of Suffolk, on the 5th November; the eve of the State Opening of Parliament. He was arrested, hung, drawn and quartered, and we've been celebrating his failure every year since! The hall is at the end of a track just past the pub.

Fame of a different kind was bestowed on the monk Bartholomew, also of Cotton Hall, who before his death in 1298, wrote three volumes of *Historia Anglicana*. If anyone ever felt like setting this tome to music, they could look around the Mechanical Music Museum Trust, on the edge of the village, for inspiration. Inside is a unique collection of musical items including music boxes, polyphons, organettes, street pianos, barrel organs, a gigantic cafe organ, wurlitzer and a theatre pipe organ, along with a musical Christmas tree and chamber pot. It is open on Sunday afternoons during the summer.

It's a shame there is no museum of village life to record when there were two shoemakers, two pork butchers (the pigs were slaughtered in an open shed), a seedman, post office and three pubs here. At least the beamed 15th century Trowel and Hammer inn has survived from the time when Sir John Paston, of Paston letters fame, was lord of the manor. The 'Paston Letters', written between Margaret Paston, John and other members of the family spanning three generations, form a vivid record of daily life at Castle Caister in Norfolk during the Wars of the Roses (1455-85), and remain one of the most important social documents of the period.

COVEHITHE

—— This was a busy port, until the sea swallowed it up. There are few more graphic illustrations of coastal erosion than here. Stray too close to the cliff-edge and barriers bar your path further. But they don't detract from the sheer natural beauty of the place, all but abandoned save for the remains of the once splendid St Andrew's church and a smattering of hides for intrepid twitchers.

St Andrew's used to be an impressive example of English Perpendicular, rivalling nearby Blythburgh, but now only the tower and tall walls remain of the original building, which suffered at the hands of the Puritan Dowsing in 1644. The font

Sea erosion at Covehithe.

was defaced, figures broken, stained glass windows smashed, while as his diary records, his band of destructive warriors 'brake down 200 pictures'.

But it was the villagers themselves who finally dismantled it bit by bit and sold the pieces off, when the dwindling community could no longer maintain it. In its place, inside the old walls, a small red brick thatched 'church within a church' was built, in 1672. The five original church bells remain, and St Andrew's is now maintained by the Redundant Churches' Fund. The sheep grazing contentedly within the remains of the 15th century fabric, and the sailors far out to sea for whom the 100 foot tower is a beacon on their journey home to Southwold, are eternally grateful.

In 1495 John Bale, compiler of the first bibliography of English literature, was born here. He was persecuted for his Protestant views but was later to become Bishop of Ossory. He was known as 'Bilious Bale' because he had such a sharp tongue. He must have attended St Andrew's in its medieval heyday. Surely even he kept silent and just wondered at its beauty.

CRETINGHAM

—— I don't know if you should ever judge somewhere by its golf club, but this one must rank as the most unpretentious with signs for a 'Bun on the Run', while you prepare to tee-off, a welcome sight. The club stands away from the hub of this pretty Deben enclave where the Grade II listed St Peter's church is almost listing inside. Or at least the walls give that impression. Maybe it is the magnificent triple-decker pulpit or the peal of five bells causing it to heel.

The bells would have tolled at midnight on 1st October 1887 when the church curate, Arthur Gilbert-Cooper, slit the throat of the vicar, Reverend William Farley, with a razor. The inquest was held at the 16th century, beamed Bell Inn (Cretingham Bell) and the local jury found the curate guilty, but of unsound mind. Some now believe he was showing the effects of the malaria he had suffered as a child in India. He was sent to Broadmoor for 40 years under the new Criminal Lunacy Act.

Following the murder the vicar's wife Harriet disappeared, adding fuel to speculation that she was in some way connected with her husband's killing. Was she having an affair with Gilbert-Cooper? A picture of the vicarage signed by Fredrick Farley, the vicar's eldest son, was found at an Essex auction with the name 'Mrs Farley, Howley Lane'. Is this where she ended up? (See *The Cretingham Murder* by Sheila Hardy.)

CROWFIELD

—— All Saints is hidden in a small copse about a mile away from the village standing, as one visitor described it in 1824, 'in a retired situation not to be seen until within a few yards of it'. To the right of the path leading up to the church gate is one lone house, and to the left, almost hidden in the undergrowth, is a fairly substantial moated area of land with a single bridge-crossing. This might have been the site of the old Crowfield Hall which burned down in the 15th century. Its larger replacement was pulled down in the 19th century, but the old stables live on in the present hall.

The church is unique in its timber-framed chancel, with glorious stained glass windows, and has been compared to a half-timbered Tudor cottage. It has also been likened to similar

The timber-framed chancel at Crowfield.

churches in Cheshire. There are neat tombstones either side of the entrance and fields all around where crows pick away at the land. All very tranquil. There were some 400 churches in Suffolk in the year 1000 – one for every 50 people (now there are 500) and it is likely that there was a wooden Saxon building here then. The church was not mentioned in the Domesday survey as this was only concerned with land or stock and if a church didn't own land, it was excluded.

To the north of Church Road is an area marked on the map as Crowfield Green. In the middle of the 19th century it consisted of several cottages and allotments, and villagers irrigated their land with water from the village pump and ponds which were usually stagnant. Legend has it that a horse fell into the Jubilee Pond at the junction of Ipswich Road and Stone Street, and drowned. Apparently it didn't make much difference to the quality of the water. No wonder pond-pox was rife at one time. The lucky ones collected filtered water from the old Bell pub.

CULFORD

—— The Culford Hall estate used to cover around 10,000 acres. Sir Nicholas Bacon, stepbrother of the Elizabethan politician Francis Bacon, built the original hall in 1591. It then passed through marriage to the Cornwallis family. The present house was said to be built for the Marquess Cornwallis in the late 1790s to a design by architect James Wyatt. It was altered beyond recognition at the turn of the last century, like so many other fine Suffolk homes. It would be nice to think the amateur artist Sir Nathaniel Cornwallis might have recorded the original hall for the benefit of future Cornwallises.

It is doubtful Charles Cornwallis ever crossed its portals. Charles was an army commander of some note. When the American War of Independence broke out he secured a victory at Camden, South Carolina, in 1780 but on 17th October 1781 he was forced to surrender his entire army to the American force at Yorktown, Virginia, sealing the independence of the American colonies. Not to be down-hearted, in 1786 he was appointed Governor-General of India and a decade later joined the vice-royalty of Ireland as Lord Lieutenant, but resigned in 1801 because of the King's refusal to grant Catholic emancipation. He negotiated the Peace of Amiens in 1802, and three years later he returned to India as Governor-General, but died shortly after arriving in the colony.

Around the time India was securing her independence from Britain, Culford Hall was being sold off, with the Forestry Commission purchasing the lion's share. The Methodist Education Committee bought the hall and park, which they converted into a school, which continues today. The church of St Mary, rebuilt in 1857, stands in the hall grounds where Humphry Repton worked his magic. At the base of the tower a bust of Sir Nathaniel, with painter's palette, languishes in the corner. The graceful chimney atop Chimney Mills (so called because it used steam as well as water), on the river Lark, would have made another good subject for him.

DALHAM

The approach from Gazeley is through a green tunnel of every imaginable tree species, opening into an expanse of thatched and flint cottages with a brook running the entire length of this exquisite hamlet. Newmarket is close by, yet there are more links with brewers than horses. The Oast House standing like a stone beehive at the village centre would seem to prove that point. Turning left at the church sign takes you down another avenue of trees to St Mary's, surely without serious

The Oast House, Dalham.

competition in the 'most wonderful of settings' stakes. A memorial to Sir Martin Stuteville (who lived in Dalham in the 17th century) in St Mary's tells how he 'saw the new world with Sir Francis Drake'. When he gained his land legs, Stuteville was also responsible for replacing the 14th century church spire with a tower in 1627, when it fell down.

The church stands above the village, next to Dalham Hall. 'Private' signs at the entrance to the hall deter uninvited guests, but footpaths leading across the fields give you a chance to look back and wonder. The original hall was built in 1704 under the watchful eye of Bishop Symon Patrick, who ordered the builders to keep working until he could see his cathedral at Ely. This was possible until 1957 when a fire led to the removal of the top floor. During its history the hall has been owned by the Duke of Wellington and Sir Cecil Rhodes, who visited although never stayed a night here.

The former village postmistress, now in her eighties, told me a story of when Rhodes, desperate for news of London, hurried into the churchyard via the hall garden and offered her father, the church stonemason, half a crown (a tidy sum in 1898) for his copy of the *Daily Express*. Rhodes' brother had the local village hall erected in Cecil's memory.

DALLINGHOO

—— The village can claim to contain what was once the smallest parish in England, Dallinghoo Wield, consisting of 34 acres. The 1980 boundary commission thought it was an anachronism and decided to get rid of it despite a heated public debate. It used to be in the south-west corner centred on four fields. A tithe map of 1841 called it 'extra parochial'. The tithes went to the Bishop of Norwich but he wouldn't have been able to dine out on the proceeds. There have never been any residents or buildings in the Wield; the Register of Electors had 'none' written across it.

The original St Mary's church was built at the time of the Norman Conquest and was served by the monks of nearby Letheringham Abbey. The tower is now in the east end of the church, but was originally in the centre until it was struck by lightning in the 17th century. Francis Light, the illegitimate son of a maid from the hall, was baptised in the church on 15th December 1740, and registered as the son of Mary Light and Incognito. Even though he was born on the wrong side of the sheets, he joined the East India Company and annexed the island of Penang in 1780, hoisting the British flag on the island on 11th August 1786, 'in the name of his Britannic Majesty and for the use of the honourable East India Company'. He named it Prince of Wales Island.

One historian has said that Light found Penang 'a jungle and left it a garden'. He was tireless in his efforts, planting pepper vines, nutmeg, cinnamon and sugar cane. He lived on a small estate he called Suffolk but turned native and married a Malay girl. His son William was sent to England to be cared for and educated by his friends, the Doughtys of grand Theberton Hall.

DARSHAM

—— Traffic thundering along the A12 from Saxmundham to Darsham, past the cafe, over the level crossing to the garage beyond, could be forgiven for thinking there is not much point hanging around to investigate further. But head seawards at the Darsham Street turn, and you will be transported into an altogether different scene. One of thatched cottages and grand houses, flanked by quiet lanes offering a perfect escape to the sea through acres of arable farmland. Established deer paths still criss-cross the landscape in this 'place of the deer'.

At one time leaving the village was not on most villagers' agenda. Two centuries ago, Darsham was a 'closed village', where everyone worked for one of the two estates belonging to the Bedingfield and Purves families, and worshipped at the pretty Primitive Methodist church with its conservatory-style frontage. The original Darsham Hall was burned down and rebuilt in 1600 by the Bedingfield family who could list among their luminaries Sir Thomas Bedingfield, a judge under Charles I. Fortunately he didn't meet the same fate as his king, and there is a memorial statue to him in the large, Norman All Saints' church.

The Purves family built Darsham House opposite the church in 1796. The grand iron gates at the front of the lane leading down to the house are sometimes open and you can sneak a look at the Early Georgian features before the 'Private' sign bars you from exploring further. Left out of the gates is a line of pretty cottages, some with entrance doors hardly bigger than those of a child's doll's house, culminating in a fine redbrick pile with a stunning sundial, clearly visible on the side. Turning right takes you to the beginning of Low Road which is said to be stalked by the 'Grey Lady' on her way from the vicarage, past Darsham House to the graveyard opposite.

🌿 DEBACH

―――― This village certainly has a spread-out feeling. For some it is a gentle assault on the senses. Robert Arib remarks on the 'fresh clean smell of a clover field at Debach' in his moving account of his time here during the Second World War when the airfield was built: 'It was a tremendous job, unknown to the world at large, except perhaps a few farmers who lived in its precincts and who watched, almost in awe, the steady stream of trucks, the upheaval of the local scenery ... a heavy bomber aerodrome, built by American labour, somewhere in eastern England' (*Here We Are Together*).

The airfield has since been turned over to agricultural land and a small industrial site with the B1078 Clopton road running through it. During the war it was home to a Class A heavy bomber station of the USAAF 493rd Bomb Group. This was the last station to become operational, as its first mission was on D-Day, 6th June 1944. But at the time it was a splendid feat of engineering which would not have been lost on Osborne Reynolds (1842-1912), a distinguished professor of engineering, who was born into a family of three generations of Debach rectors.

All Saints House is now private, but was a church and the small graveyard in front is still evident; which is fitting. In 1813 the Reverend Roberts, whose family were rectors here from 1779 to 1850, built his home in the parish church. In the present one, the Stars and Stripes hangs above a new commemorative board listing the men from the USAAF who lost their lives while stationed 'somewhere in eastern England'.

🌿 DEBENHAM

―――― This is the source of the Deben, in an area known as High Suffolk where the feudal enclosures of this Anglo-Saxon 'deopan hamme' fill up with flowers in the spring and spill over with water in the winter. If you fancy a splashing time, Water Lane and The Wash should satisfy.

The heavy moisture-retaining clay soil gives some of the largest yields of barley and wheat in the world. The Chevallier strain of barley, which used to be exported to North America, was first grown here in the 1820s after a farm labourer noticed a huge ear of barley stuck to his shoe. He planted the seed from it in his garden and the following year showed the result to his landlord, Dr Chevallier (see also Aspall). This successful strain has only recently been supplanted by modern (dare we mention) genetically-engineered varieties.

Away from the fields, the main street runs north to south, rising gently with a mix of lovely properties. At the north-east the c.1500 former Guildhall has a four-centred door-arch and brick-nogging on the upper floor. The nave of St Mary Magdalene with its massive timber roof is almost like an upturned ship (*navis* is the Latin for ship, as in navy). The Rev John Simson, apothecary of Debenham is buried here. On his death in 1697, he left a perpetual charge on land in Debenham to provide bread, every Sunday, for poor families. Could this be why the second Debenham cookery book has recently been published?

There is a tomb in the church of Sir Charles and Lady Framlingham who lived at Crows Hall around the time of the Spanish Armada. There is also a plaque in memory of Sir Charles Gawdy, a relation of the Framlinghams and later resident of Crows Hall. He was a staunch Royalist and was besieged at the hall during the Civil War. All that remains of the original 14th century hall is the gatehouse and part of the north wing hidden away a mile to the south-east on the north side of the Cretingham road. There are between 500 and 600 moated farmsteads, or halls, in Suffolk mostly dating from the 12th to 15th centuries when the moats were dug for drainage, important on this heavy clay soil.

DENNINGTON

———— An old man tending his allotment told me how sad he was that there is little in the village now to boast about. The chapel closed last June, and there are some dilapidated buildings around. The 15th century Queen's Head has some pretty cottages as company and on the green opposite is the new post office. The old Victorian one, on the road to the right of the pub, has a pretty stained glass porch.

There used to be a Druid temple on an ancient way, running north to south, near the site of the Perpendicular-style church, which is a true treasure trove. Some say it is unrivalled in the county for the variety of interesting and beautiful artefacts it contains. The view down the length of the church (some 130 feet)

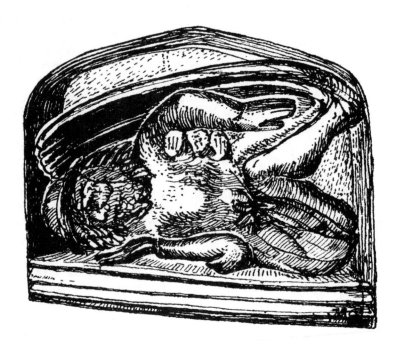

A Sciapod carved in a bench end in Dennington church.

is glorious. The woodwork is mostly medieval and in one bench end (centre aisle, south, sixth from west) is a Sciapod, shielding himself from the sun with his enormous foot. These creatures are normally seen in African art and this is the only example of its kind in an English church. Sciapod comes from the Greek meaning 'shade foot' and Herodotus, the Greek historian, records the creature as coming from the 'dark continent'; perhaps Libya.

There is also a magnificent tomb of Lord Bardolph, Knight of the Garter, who fought at Agincourt with Henry V. He is depicted dressed in armour and lying alongside him, his wife Lady Joan. As treasurer to Henry's household, he is said to have managed the great King's funeral after his premature death, at 35, from dysentery. For his own funeral (he died in 1441) Bardolph laid down that there was to be no pomp and ceremony; only 20 burning torches when his corpse passed through the county's towns.

DITCHINGHAM

—— Now we're in border country, and as Ditchingham, on the banks of the Waveney, is geographically linked more with the nearby town of Bungay, than with Norfolk, we can just about get away with including it! Just to the north-east on Broome Heath is a Neolithic (3250-1800 BC) long barrow, and an excavation in 1970 uncovered a settlement to the south-west.

Artefacts from a bygone age are certainly things the writer and Egyptologist Sir Henry Rider Haggard (1856-1925) could identify with. He lived at Georgian Ditchingham House, once dubbed 'mustard pot hall' because of the shape of its chimney pots, when his wife inherited the farm in 1880. He was a prolific writer producing more than 50 books, including his epic adventure stories *Cleopatra* and *King Solomon's Mines*. Apparently his friend Rudyard Kipling was rather envious of his ability to churn out the tomes.

While at Ditchingham, Haggard wrote his famous diary *A Farmer's Year* and devised agricultural reforms which were considered at the time to be too radical for the then Conservative Party (for which he was standing as a candidate), but quickly became the farmer's bible. He died in 1925 and is buried in the churchyard of the 15th century St Mary's where a window was installed in his memory by his daughter Lilias, who was no mean writer herself and a renowned observer of Norfolk Life.

DUNWICH

—— The romantically-minded still hold that you can hear the bells of the lost churches ringing under the sea when the wind is blowing in the right direction; whatever the right direction is. Recent waves pounding the coast have revealed more of its sunken treasures.

When Felix came over from Burgundy in AD 630 to establish the first Christian See of East Anglia at a place called 'Domnoc', thought to be Dunwich (although some believe it to be Felixstowe), the coastline was at least one mile further out to sea. There was also a large harbour at the mouth of the river Blyth.

Dunwich's prosperity as a port probably reached its height in the 13th century when it covered approximately one square mile and had eight churches. Records from the reign of Edward I

(1272-1307) give some indication of its size with a shipping list that included eleven ships of war, 36 trading ships and 24 fishing smacks. During the great storm of 1287, which caused so much damage at the Cinque Ports further south, Dunwich had its first real taste of what was to come and much of the harbour was damaged. A subsequent, more violent storm in 1328 blocked the harbour mouth causing a second to form one mile further north and in 1342, 400 houses were lost.

In spite of losing half of the city to the sea, Dunwich still returned two members to Parliament, had three lifeboats and sent six warships to the siege of Calais in 1359. Further silting of the river caused a gradual northward shift benefiting Walberswick and Southwold. At the same time the sea was eating into the shoreline, which it has continued to do ever since. By the early 18th century no more than a memory was left of its greatness, which was not helped by the great storm of 1740 which according to an historical account: 'blew for several days and occasioned terrible devastations'.

The last of its churches was abandoned in 1755, finally slipping into the sea in 1919. A buttress from the church was moved away and set up as a memorial to the lost town in the modern (c.1830) churchyard of St James.

EARL SOHAM

——— I have often admired Tudor, moated Earl Soham lodge, set back from the street, with its Georgian windows. The earl in question is Roger de Bigod, Earl of Norfolk. The 'soham' refers to a settlement by a lake. There is an unusual feature in this particular old Roman route connecting Peasenhall with Coddenham; a twist in an otherwise straight highway. The reason for this was to find a way around the large lake. The original road passed between the lodge and the village street.

Fish might not appear as much as it should in modern diets, but in the Middle Ages it was a staple. This plentiful source of essential vitamins was probably bred at the lodge, or brought over from Framlingham, cleaned and then stored in a reedy lake, or stew pond, behind what is now the Baptist chapel. The lake was drained around 1970 and the succession of Georgian-fronted houses and cottages lining one side of the street now have their back to it. It was quite substantial and thus shared with neighbouring Monk Soham.

More weaving about is required at the west of the village, where the road skirts around the edge of the eye-catching village sign, which has a carved wooden figure of a falconer with a hawk on his arm. This magnificent work was carried out by the Ipswich School of Art and highlights how, in medieval times, the village was a falconry centre. The carving contrasts well with some of the grotesque figures in the 13th century church.

By the 1780s, smuggling was the number one pursuit. Surgeon and farmer William Goodwin, who lived in Street Farm House just off the main village green, kept a diary (now in Ipswich Record Office) of all the goings-on connected with this illegal, but highly profitable, trade. A huge number of horses and carts were used to collect the contraband which was sometimes hidden in the local churches en route inland from the coast; including St Mary's.

EARL STONHAM

—— So is this the site of the lost Roman village of Sitomagus? A number of Roman remains, embracing a period of 400 years, have been found here including coins and pottery. Sitomagus was on the Antonines Itinerary, a sort of AA guide of its day. The antiquarian, and former local schoolmaster, H. Whatling looked at the mileage between the major Roman towns of Combretovium (Coddenham) and Venta Icenorum (Caistor St Edmund) and worked out that this should be the spot. However, modern archaeologists don't seem to agree with him. He was also a keen artist and some of his drawings can be seen in Christchurch Mansion, Ipswich.

What is certain is that the thatched Yew Tree House in Forward Green, as you head for Stowmarket, has survived unaltered, since the mid 15th century. It was the old post office and forge and until a few years ago, had been standing empty for a quarter of a century, the interior almost frozen in time. When the new owners moved in they found an old post office counter and a postman's hat from 1923. When the Runacles family ran the postal service, it was quite a spectacle, I believe. The kitchen doubled up as the office, so stamps were often scattered among the vegetables.

Middlewood Green and Brood Green, along with Forward, make up the greens, enclosed in the 1820s, which were supposed to provide allotments for the poor of the parish to grow their vegetables. There are still some allotments in front of the Parish Room, built next to the church in 1899, as a gift to the villagers from the wife of a former rector. It is a good example of the pre-fab wooden buildings built by Boulton and Paul of Norwich who were the masters of pre-fab of their day. Now villagers use it to sew in, read in, or contemplate in.

EASTON

——— The home of the 'crinkle-crankle' wall. Alongside the path leading to the south porch and bordering three sides of the churchyard is part of the wavy wall erected around the 150 acres of Easton Park by the 5th Earl of Rochford around 1830. It's supposed to be the longest of its kind in the world. There could be as many as 60 of these brick-built constructions, also known as ribbons or serpentines, in the county. Did they originate in Holland? The nooks formed along the walls are great for growing fruit in kitchen gardens. They are also rather nice to look at and I wish my garden could accommodate one. Sadly there have been a few chinks in the Earl's brick armour, allowing new houses to take root where the mansion once stood; built by Sir Anthony Wingfield, 1st Baronet, around 1552. It was demolished in 1923, but some of the estate buildings remain. A thatched dovecote in the grounds is octagonal on the outside but circular inside, with a round cupola. I wouldn't mind one of those either!

James Clarke would not be too impressed by the changing scene. He is buried in the broadly 13th century church, which lies on a hill set amongst magnificent trees. Clarke, who was a shopkeeper for many years, died in 1861 and was one of Suffolk's noted antiquarians. His book *Suffolk Antiquary* describes, among other things, the travels of William Dowsing whose family lived here at one time.

On the road to Hacheston, is the present Glevering Hall, built between 1786 and 1794 by John White the elder, possibly with design input from Andrew Archdeckne, when he wasn't acting as Queen Anne's attorney in Jamaica. The mansion has been described as one of the best Georgian houses in Suffolk. Park in front to admire the grounds laid out by Humphry Repton and discussed in his sketches from the period.

EDWARDSTONE

────── What is encased in crimson and studded with gilded suns? Part of an organ built by Father Smith in 1671 for the Sheldonian Theatre in Oxford and said to be the oldest Father Smith machine in the country. When it gets going, hold onto your hats. If the nine chandeliers in the church held glass, they would probably shatter. They once held 96 candles and were modified to take light bulbs after 1957 when electricity was piped in.

The bells were derelict until 1986 and the leading light in their restoration was Sarah Titford, vicar's wife. One of her ways of raising money was to charter Concorde for the day on 20th November, St Edmund's Day. Booming noises again!

Which is at odds with the peaceful feel of this village of nearly 2,000 acres lying in the old Cosford Hundred on a plateau 60 metres above sea level. The old hall has gone but the park is still lovely with views across the distant meadows of the Box valley. A fine red brick archway with an adjoining lodge stands at the entrance to the park and church, and is known hereabouts as 'Temple'. It was built around 1840 and as its name indicates, is believed to be modelled on the original Temple Bar in London, now re-erected in Hertfordshire.

ELMSETT

────── I decided to sit on the church bench to take in the view over a valley of gently rolling hills. The 13th century church of St Peter dates back to Norman times and guards a scene little changed since Thomas Gainsborough painted it in 1750. Just one change. As I was informed by one resident, 'there are more fields now than when the protest was'.

The protest to which she was referring happened in 1934. It is recorded in the 1935 Tithe Memorial opposite the church, and commemorates the villagers' fight against the antiquated tithe tax that had become totally unjust by the 1930s. The lorries attempting to collect the 'dues' of furniture from Elmsett Hall, including a baby's bed and blankets, a herd of dairy cows, eight corn and seed stacks, valued at £1,200 for a tithe of £385, were turned back by the crowds. Several large elms were felled and blocked the farm entrance.

The moated rectory, now a private house, was once home to John Bois, one of the 54 scholars involved in the translation of the

King James' Bible which was commissioned by James I in 1604. The scholars worked in groups at Oxford, Cambridge and Westminster and by 1611, they were able to present the King with the Good Book: 'that inestimable treasure which excelleth all the riches of the earth'. Since its completion, it has become the most widely read work in the English language.

ELVEDEN

────── The three parishes of Elveden, Eriswell and Icklingham meet on the Elveden estate where the magnificent Corinthian column, topped by a Grecian urn, looms 127 feet above. The 1921 structure was designed by Clyde Young and originally dedicated to the local men who lost their lives in the First World War. Ironic really as this Breckland village was the setting for the early days of tank warfare training. Now it is the setting for some of the longest traffic queues in the county along the A11. Those in the know take the parallel route through farmland, which probably doesn't please the farmer too much.

Duleep Singh, the Maharajah of the Sikhs, seems to have upset a few people himself. In 1856 he was banished from India for life and moved to the Georgian country house at Elveden Hall, eventually converting the building into an Oriental palace rich in marble, with a large copper dome. He had six children who after the Maharajah's death, settled in the Thetford area. The whereabouts of Princess Bamba, Princess Catherine and Princess Sophia Alexandra are unclear. Maybe they swapped Suffolk for India? The hall was once the greatest shooting estate in Britain and the Maharajah was one of the best shots around. In *Memoirs of a Gamekeeper*, the author Turner suggests why: 'Perhaps there was something in these Indian potentates' breeding that gave them such extraordinary quick sight and power of movement.' Quite so.

In 1894 the Guinness family moved into the hall, transforming it into an Edwardian palace, no doubt to make guests such as Edward VII feel at home. Attempts were also made to re-establish the great bustard in the grounds, which were famous for their game birds. The hall hadn't been lived in for 20 years and its distinction in the last few has been as one of the locations for Stanley Kubrick's last film, *Eyes Wide Shut*. If you kept your eyes closed you might miss some of the glories of the Norman church which received the same lavish treatment as the hall from both the Maharajah and the Earl, including decoration with ornate Art Nouveau ornaments.

ERISWELL

—— Before the canal relieved pressure on the river Lark, Eriswell used to flood frequently. The lady who kindly showed me around the church recalled when the pump would be going during funerals to stop St Peter's from disappearing under water!

In 1649 the New England Company bought the manor of Eriswell to provide income from tenant farmers to send missionaries to North America to teach the native Indians Christianity. The initials N.E.C can be seen on the village hall, originally built as a school, and on a number of houses in the village. In 1869 the Society sold the manor to the Maharajah Duleep Singh and in 1894, it was bought by the Guinness family whose head is the Earl of Iveagh.

In 1818 a young North American Indian boy was sent over from the USA to be educated at the school. A new headstone to James Paul, apprenticed to Thomas Houghton carpenter and builder for only two years, is outside by the porch.

Eriswell Warren became important from the 13th century when rabbits were farmed for their meat and fur. The name Warren, after which the fields were named, derives from this industry. During the Napoleonic Wars, the Warren supplied up to 25,000 rabbits a year to feed hungry London. The warreners lived in a low, fortified tower to protect them from armed poachers, and stones from it can be seen in buildings such as High Lodge. The quaint cottages opposite the Warren are known as 'Little London'. I asked why. 'We think it is because they are so tightly packed together,' was the reply. And they certainly are, although I imagine the property prices do not compare.

ERWARTON

—— From the lowlands of Holbrook we come to the comparative highlands, with dips down to the water's edge. A track opposite the pub leads down a bumpy lane with a splendid view left to Felixstowe, and right to Harwich for some serious ferry spotting.

The south side of the church offers a sweep over the Stour

estuary. Quite a few materials were used to build it including brick, dressed stone, flint, pebbles and large amounts of chunky brown septaria, the local cement-like material dug from nearby beaches, or dredged out of the river. The tower has one bell cast by Charles Newman in 1700. It is said that five other bells were removed during the Civil War, and their metal turned into ammunition to defend Erwarton Hall against attack from General Sir Thomas Fairfax's Parliamentary soldiers.

The hall has an Elizabethan facade, but dates from an earlier period. The gatehouse, which stands immediately in front of the hall (you cannot miss it), is an impressive tunnel-vaulted red brick structure with nine pinnacles, built in 1549. The story goes that Elizabeth I's mother, Anne Boleyn, stayed here while courting Henry VIII and left a lasting legacy.

Henry's second wife, who was to lose her head in 1536, lost her heart, figuratively speaking, to the King from the outset of their relationship. The resting place for her vital organ is said to be the church chancel; a view given more credence with the discovery, during the 19th century alterations to the church, of a heart-shaped lead casket. Joseph Amner, who died in 1874 having been sacristan of the church for 50 years, was a witness and recalled the moment when the stonemasons found 'a leaden box covered with lime ... inside there was only a little black dust. It was soldered up again and placed in a coffin in the vault of the Lady Chapel'.

EXNING

—— The first Norman Earl of East Anglia, Ralph Wader, was married here in 1076. Wader plotted a rebellion against his Norman kinsmen and was subsequently defeated and outlawed. A century later, Matthew, Count of Boulogne, divided Exning among four of his noblemen and it remained split until the 17th century when the whole estate was taken over by the Cotton family, who lived at Landwade. The family name appears in the church of St Martin which is mainly 14th century but is said to have been founded by St Felix during a visit to the court of King Anna in AD 636.

While here, he baptised the three royal princesses: Ethelreda, who founded Ely Cathedral; Sexburgha, who married the King of Kent; and Wendred, in the group of springs known as St Mindred's Well. The name is probably a corruption of 'St

Wendred'. I should say there was a certain scepticism when I mentioned the holy well on my visit and no one could actually direct me to the spot. Some say the springs dried up in 1985, although the likely site is an overgrown pond on private ground near the school playing fields. I can't imagine the present vicar getting away with using the muddy water for his baptism, as his predecessors were said to do!

Wendred apparently built up a vast knowledge of herbs and medicines. While there is no existing proof of her performing any miracles, she put her knowledge to good use using the waters from the spring for bathing the wounds of injured people and animals. I wonder how good she was at catching eels? The stream running through the village used to provide an annual catch of over 8,000 of the slimy creatures.

EYE

In 1636, Nicholas Bedingfield built almshouses for four poor widows of the town, providing them with two shillings monthly, a new grey gown every two or three years and two cartloads of firewood annually. What the Suffragettes would have made of such masculine beneficence is hard to say.

From the beginning of the 1920s, six sisters lived at the 17th century Linden House that was encased in brick in the early 18th century. One of them, Margaret Thompson, pushed the cause of women and was imprisoned three times for her trouble between 1909 and 1912. She even managed to share a cell with the leading light of the Suffragette Movement, Emmeline Pankhurst, who with younger daughter Christabel founded the Women's Social and Political Union in 1903 calling for voting rights to women. A campaign which was to ruffle a few feathers.

When William Malet built his castle between 1066 and 1071, he was asking for trouble. It withstood attack by Hugh Bigod in 1173 and was probably at its peak after being rebuilt in 1182. During the 13th century, it fell into decline and a post mill was built in the ruins in 1560, curiously followed by the town workhouse from 1794.

Little of the original Guildhall remains either, except for the carved Archangel Gabriel on the corner post. Used as Eye school from 1495 until the 20th century, it taught the seven 'sciences': Grammar, Logic, Rhetoric, Arithmetic, Music, Geometry and Astronomy. Simple arithmetic would suggest that around £1m is needed to restore the once grand town hall, erected at the height of Victorian prosperity. The building originally cost only £2,500 and was part-financed by Sir Edward Kerrison, a wealthy MP and local landowner, in the 1850s when Eye was a thriving market town. Plans are afoot to make the town hall sparkle again.

EYKE

—— An oak forest (now Staverton Forest – see Butley) extended almost to the river marshes a thousand years ago. The time when wood and wattle huts stood on rising ground above the river valley where springs provided water. You can still just about trace a track from the Saxon burial site at Sutton, via the ford at Wilford, continuing through Bromeswell on to lower Eyke. King John held the Staverton lands before his accession in 1199, which would explain the forest's other name, King John's Park.

A unique feature of the village is a replica of the parish key, which hangs on the north wall of the church nave; the original, from the 15th century, is in the V&A. The head of the key is shaped into the word 'IKE', an early spelling of the name. It is fair to say the church does not stand on a great site in a pretty village. The interior is more interesting though with much of the woodwork, including the font cover, locally crafted in a class run by Archdeacon Darling in the 1930s.

During the height of the Peasants' Revolt, local labourers joined in enthusiastically breaking down the home of John of Staverton. In 1587, the parishioners were at it again, this time the bogeyman was Thomas Seckford, benefactor of Woodbridge, who took offence at the felt hats, introduced from Germany, being worn on Sundays instead of English hats made from pile. He talked punitive fines.

The nearby American airbase closed in 1993, which meant an end to low-flying aircraft; something the locals have got used to over the years. In 1940, a German seaplane crashed in the garden of Eyke House leaving a huge crater. The crew survived. No one mentioned the hats!

FELIXSTOWE

—— Blue plaques are set to go up in this resort to mark the homes of famous former residents. Ripe for inclusion would have been Wallis Simpson's old hideaway, Beach House in Undercliff Road East, where she stayed for six weeks during the 1936 Abdication crisis. This was so she could secure a residential qualification for her divorce from her American husband, Ernest, at Ipswich, allowing her to marry Edward. The King visited her frequently, landing his red plane on the cliffs of old Felixstowe. Sadly, the five-bedroomed house has been demolished, which would have pleased Wallis who considered it 'cramped'. She also claimed local people ignored her. Now tea-rooms, a stone's throw from her old house, have been named in her honour.

The barrack huts at the port where the airman Shaw, better known as T. E. Lawrence of Arabia, lived while serving at the Marine Aircraft Experimental Establishment are long gone. And all that is left in Colneis Road of Walton Old Hall, where Edward III stayed while gathering a mighty battle fleet to attack France in 1338, is a pile of knee-high ruins.

Sir John Mills began his acting career at St John's Hall, Princes Road, which remains. South Beach mansion, the stunning white Italianate villa, will always hold a prominent place in the town's history as the building the Empress of Germany stayed at in 1891 when she put Felixstowe on the map as a seaside resort. It was built in 1865 for Charles Eley, a cartridge manufacturer, and notable guests included King Madel of Portugal. Douglas Tollemache, of the locally renowned Tollemache family, lived here and his family crest remains in stained glass in a magnificent window over the Victorian staircase.

The fishing hamlet of Felixstowe Ferry is in danger of disappearing if defences continue to crumble. The pavilion, with origins dating back to 1930, is today almost at the mercy of the sea.

FELSHAM & COCKFIELD

—— You could be forgiven for overlooking this village, crammed as it is among beet fields to the south-east of Bury St Edmunds. But if you did, you would miss out on what's hidden away behind Mausoleum House (third left past the church with iron gates outside).

In a field at the back of the house are the remains of a square-bricked tomb, built around 1755 by one Mr John Reynolds for his only child (the tomb gets a mention in John Wesley's *Journal*). According to folklore, Reynolds Senior decided to build the mausoleum after a long dispute with the rector of St Peter's; it seems he didn't want the church to benefit from his family's funeral expenses. The bodies were eventually moved to the churchyard and only a few bricks of the tomb remain in place; the rest were plundered by locals for their new homes.

Thatched Moore's Farm is living testament to former owner Stanley Steadman's equally independent spirit. Over the years he has turned the farm into a celebration of art, with over 100 paintings ranging in subjects from Windsor Castle to the Scottish glens. Stanley doesn't live there any more but you can still see some of his paintings in the brickwork of the barn on the edge of the road. The farm is past Lower Green taking the left-hand fork. The post office is always willing to help with directions.

At nearby Cockfield, Dr Churchill Babbington, the uncle of author Robert Louis Stevenson, lived in the Rectory on one side of the green. On one of his visits to his uncle, he wrote *Treasure Island*. Well, the opening paragraphs, perhaps. Apparently he based the character 'Long John Silver', on local man Peg Leg Brinkley.

🌿 FLIXTON

—— You don't normally find aviation parks behind pubs, so be prepared to feast your eyes on Gloster Javelins, North American F-1000 Super Sabres and big brutes like a Vickers Valetta which small and big kids alike can clamber over (open April-October; reduced times during winter). The 'Bungay Buckeroos', members of the 446th Bomb Group who served here during the war, and who are remembered in the largely Victorian church, would surely be delighted.

The church tower is said to be a faithful copy of the original, which fell in 1835. The spire, with Germanic lozenge-shaped broaches, is unique to East Anglia. Uphill from St Mary's, near the Abbey Farmhouse, you can still see a small section of the 13th century Augustinian priory. Three centuries later, the Tasburgh family who lived at St Peter's Hall, which dates from 1280, used architectural salvage from the priory to extend their hall. Caen stone can be seen in the back bar area of the hall. The adjoining brewery was built in 1996 and produces traditional beers, as well as 'unusual' ones such as honey porter and fruit beer. It was common practice up to the 19th century to add fruits and honey to beers to create special seasonal brews. (St Peter's is signposted from the village.)

Roman Catholic John Tasburgh built Flixton Hall in 1615, with just a little help from Britain's first architect, Inigo Jones. When Charles II admired the hall, he was told it belonged to a 'Popish dog'. The King's reply was said to be: 'But the dog has a very beautiful kennel!' The estate passed to the Adairs in 1753, and was eventually broken down in 1950. A former resident of the Priest's House knows all about being in the doghouse. The eponymous Captain Boycott of County Mayo, after whom the expression 'to boycott' was coined (after the treatment he received from his neighbours in Ireland in 1880), died there in 1897.

FRAMLINGHAM

—— Walking along the castle parapets gives you an instant grasp of royal times past. In 1553, Catholic Mary Tudor ('Bloody Mary') took refuge in the castle when the Protestant supporters of Lady Jane Grey attempted to take the throne, and was subsequently proclaimed Queen by her supporters before marching on London. A couple of centuries earlier, Mary could have elected to go by boat to Greenwich, catching a lift on one of the small ships plying the tiny river Ore which feeds the northern end of the Mere, out to the sea at Orford.

When the Howards, Dukes of Norfolk, were in residence in the 15th century before they lost their castle (and their heads) under Henry VIII's Anglican backlash, the castle resembled a mini-Whitehall, rather than a Royal palace. A cast of hundreds toiled away within its walls, and was sustained in no small measure by the Mere, which provided such staples as fish. On the eastern side you can just make out two depressions, which used to be fish-rearing pools. The surrounding meadows were ideal for grazing deer and wildfowl.

As well as being at one time a Catholic stronghold, 'Fram' has also been a centre of dissenting views. The Unitarian church in Bridge Street, built in 1717 and still going strong, was the first meeting house of the Dissenters. Thomas Mills, Dissenter, died in 1703. As he couldn't be buried in the churchyard, he was committed to the earth in the garden of his home, Tomb House in Station Road. His sepulchral monument can't really compare to those inside St Michael's church, including the one of Henry FitzRoy, Duke of Richmond and the illegitimate son of Henry VIII (1536) and Elizabeth Blount, a lady in waiting to Catherine of Aragon.

Without wishing to dwell on burials, the town cemetery, hidden away behind brightly-painted iron gates in Double Street, is two acres of urban tranquillity and a delight when the flowers are in bloom. A rare species has made its way to the Kew Garden seed bank.

FRAMSDEN

Boundary Farm, one mile north-west, is supposed to be one of the few spots in the county where fritillaries flourish. Fritillary is a genus of the lily family, and usually has chequered purple flowers. I don't think such plants figure large in the staple diets of sheep, a herd of which (including a black one) were champing away happily, keeping the graveyard tidy, when I dropped by. The pretty detached lychgate has a sign saying: 'dogs must be kept on lead so as not to worry the sheep'. As the sheep are kept behind wire anyway I couldn't see how their stress-levels were likely to increase too much by the sight of the odd hound. But if they ever wandered inside the early 14th century St Mary's, they could conceivably get a little upset. The church has an original collection of grotesque carved figures on the stalls as well as misericords from the same period.

A footpath next to the village hall takes you through a back garden and over a bridge to the church for another look at the woolly animals, and the option of carrying on five miles north-east to Framlingham. Half a mile to the west of the village is a fine post mill, rescued from dereliction by volunteer mill enthusiasts in the late 1960s. Built in 1760, the mill was refitted in 1836, when it was raised to its present height of nearly 50 feet and is a good example of how some post mills were modernised during their life, rather than being demolished. Although one pair of sails and the fantail, for turning the mill to wind, are missing, the survival of much of the 18th century structure more than compensates.

FRESSINGFIELD

———— Pilgrims used to ride donkeys through here on their way from Dunwich to Walsingham. Which would have made a change from marauding Frisians who settled in this village, on a plateau south of the Waveney, centuries before.

The 14th century church contains some of the best examples of architecture and furnishings in the county. Alice de la Pole, who was the granddaughter of Geoffrey Chaucer, the 'Father of English Poetry' and author of *The Canterbury Tales*, added the porch in the 15th century in memory of her husband William, Duke of Suffolk and her son.

The timber framed Ufford Hall, two miles south of the village along the B1116, was lived in by the Sancroft family; Dr William Sancroft became Archbishop of Canterbury in 1677. It was a time of religious controversy with mutual distrust between Catholics and Protestants, and Sancroft performed his duties well under the Catholic James II. He was expelled from the church when he refused to take the oaths of allegiance at the accession of William and Mary in 1689. He spent time in the Tower of London and eventually returned to Fressingfield to die in 1693. His monument, a tomb-chest, stands in the churchyard.

Next to the churchyard is the former guild-house, a brick and timber building with a corner-post carving of St Margaret of Antioch, patroness of the guild. She did not exist as a person, only a character of religious fiction, and is said to have been swallowed by a dragon. Such fiery creatures are not likely to make it onto the menu of the restaurant (Fox and Goose) which operates from her former guild.

FRESTON

———— Aerial photographs have shown that there was once a causewayed camp here, and archaeological surveys have found remains dating back 4,000 years. The redbrick De Freston tower, standing high up in parkland on the west bank of the river Orwell, isn't quite so old. It is not absolutely certain why or when it was built (possibly mid-16th century) but the architect was Thomas Gooding, a prominent Elizabethan merchant from Ipswich, who could well have wanted somewhere to watch the comings and goings of his ships on the river. It once formed the corner of the tower of his manor house.

The folklore attached to it is more interesting. Legend has it that it was built as a place of study for Ellen Latimer, daughter of William Latimer, Lord de Freston. It has six floors, and Ellen apparently used each one to study a different subject, finishing

The De Freston tower.

with astronomy at the top, as this floor was open to the sky.

At the foot of Freston Hill is a building built originally as a gatehouse to Woolverstone Hall, and known locally as the 'Monkey House'. The story goes that a pet monkey saved the Berners family by alerting them about a fire. An inscription above one of the windows reads *'del fuego el avula'* – 'torn away from the fire'. For the best view of the tower, park at the Monkey House and walk down to the water (via Stoke Sailing Club), turn right and there it is with just a herd of Charolais cattle grazing at the water's edge, for company.

FRISTON

────── It is not just the distinctive mill – at 55 feet apparently the highest postmill in Europe – that makes you get a sense of the Low Countries here. A number of settlers travelled to the 'farmstead of the Frisians' in the 4th century from the lowlands of what is now Holland and Belgium. Standing somewhat morosely to the south of the village, the early 19th century mill once powered two pairs of stones in the breast, one pair in the tail, a flour dresser and an oat crusher.

Thirty years later, the Swing Riots, organised by the Suffolk wing of the Chartist Movement, were said to have started here. The peak was reached in 1843 when the Chartists' Petition to Parliament calling for the rights of working men to be recognised was rejected. The movement never became deeply rooted in Suffolk, but was strong enough for Friston to earn the epithet, 'the Suffolk Metropolis of Chartism'.

Somewhat heated meetings were held at the Chequers Inn, which was probably built at the end of the 18th century when the village started to expand. There hadn't been much need for a pub before then, as most Fristonians tried their hand at a spot of home brewing, probably feeling rather in need of their beds after quaffing the fairly lethal concoctions.

They could have retired to the 'bedroom houses'; the colloquial name for the single-storey properties dotted around the village. So called, because if ever anyone needed another room, they just built one on the side rather than above, apparently. Most of the village properties still belong to a family related to the now extinct Earldom of Strafford, the Vernon-Wentworths. Their former Victorian mansion with neo-Georgian river frontage, part of the old Blackheath estate, is a distinctive landmark along the

Alde estuary, and a location to die for. The original house was rather more flamboyant, with 50 foot high towers hiding the water tanks.

GEDDING

—— What do Rolling Stones guitarist Bill Wyman and a former MP for Suffolk have in common? Not a lot on the face of it, but they have both owned Gedding Hall at one time. Gedding Hall is a partly-moated Tudor mansion with a striking gatehouse. In 1196 Adam de Geddynge, Lord of the Manor of Geddynge and Thurmestone, had the mansion built. Alterations were made in the 15th century and then again in 1897 when it became part of an extension of the new house and had, in some minds, a monstrous brick tower added, designed by the Mayor of Leicester.

The village is essentially the hall, the church and a few farms including Grange Farm where the Red Poll dairy herd, the traditional Suffolk breed, was founded by Captain and Mrs Walmsley. The breed was very popular during the 1930s–1960s because of its ability to produce both dairy and beef products under sometimes harsh conditions.

In his *Suffolk Traveller* of 1732-4, John Kirby describes the butter they produced as being 'justly esteemed the pleasantest and best in England ... The breed is universally polled – a clean throat, with little dewlap; a snake's head; clean thin legs and short; a springing rib and a large carcass'. The Red Poll meat is evidently tender because it was never bred for pulling muscle. The Suffolk Punch was there for that. The Black Faced sheep completes the trio of animals known as the Suffolk Trinity.

GLEMSFORD

—— As you climb the winding road, spectacular Monk's Hall stares down at you, a dramatic pink and red house, half-timbered and not a building you would expect to find in a place known as 'Little Egypt'.

Why so called? One theory links it with the year 1885. Captain Henry Cooke congregated the villagers on Tye Green and led them to nearby Long Melford to exercise their voting rights for the first time. A full-scale riot broke out and troops from Bury St

Edmunds had to be called in. It was the last time the Riot Act (now Public Order Act) was read in Suffolk. The Glemsfordians were so furious they were compared with the Egyptians fighting in the Sudan at the same time.

Glemsford is certainly one of the largest villages in West Suffolk, with records dating back to Edward the Confessor. At Domesday the manor was held by Odo, Bishop of Bayeux and Earl of Champagne. He was half-brother to William the Conqueror and it was he who commissioned the Bayeux Tapestry. Perhaps the men of Glemsford should have been put to task weaving it?

Glemsford has been a weaving centre for many years and in the Middle Ages produced its own cloth called Glynforths (or Gleynforths) which were white, rather than the traditional dyed blue of the Suffolks. There was a silk throwing mill here in 1824 and silk from the mill has been woven into royal robes. The old mill (in Brook Street) is now part of a modern factory building with only the end bay and clock tower remaining.

Glemsford church stands high on the hill, crowning a ridge, with gravestones dotted below. Cardinal Wolsey's faithful servant and biographer, George Cavendish – he wrote *The Life of Cardinal Wolsey* in 1554 – is buried in the churchyard of St Mary's. He lived with his wife in Glemsford until he was 26, when he left to serve Wolsey.

GREAT & LITTLE BEALINGS

—— There is a lovely view of Great Bealings church as you enter Little Bealings from Playford; just past an old ivy-clad castellated water tower. These two villages look so comfortably settled in the Fynn valley; as if nothing short of a nuclear explosion would move them on. The Seckford family didn't move on willingly either.

Thomas Seckford acquired the family name from the nearby manor of Seckford in the 12th century. In 1505 the second Thomas Seckford inherited the estate which included the manor of Little Bealings, or Belinges Parva. He married Margaret Wingfield, a member of one of the most influential families in Suffolk, and built Seckford Hall on the Great Bealings boundary. The third, and most notable, Thomas Seckford was born here in 1515. As a younger son he wasn't entitled to inherit the property, so he moved into, and extended, the Augustinian priory in

Woodbridge which was owned by the Wingfields and is now known as the Abbey (part of Woodbridge school). No wonder Great Bealings is regarded as the 'village' of Woodbridge.

Bealings House (just under a mile east) is a beautiful, redbrick property with a history. Major Moor, author of *Suffolk Words & Phrases*, bought it on retirement from India in 1806. He apparently interred his collection of heathen idols in the folly in front of the house, so no ill would come of them. His son Edward, rector from 1844, was probably grateful he didn't leave them to him. St Mary's is set among fields and magnificent limes and was probably the chapel to Great Bealings Hall, opposite, next to a patch of grass which serves as the church car park. Sir John Major of Worlingworth Hall owned the manor in 1781, followed by daughter Anne who married Sir John Henniker. The stained glass Henniker Achievement with its crest surmounted by a Baron's coronet, can be seen in the north window of the nave.

You can walk from Great to Little Bealings, under a mile away. The old station is a reminder of the Ipswich-Lowestoft line bisecting Little Bealings, as does the Fynn winding its way to Martlesham Creek. Not quite castaway territory perhaps, but inside All Saints is a memorial to John Colvin, biographer of Robert Louis Stevenson, of *Treasure Island* fame, as well as a splendid set of embroidered kneelers and padded pews. Now there's comfort!

GREAT FINBOROUGH

—— A fine flint wall guided me into this village, three miles west of Stowmarket. It was originally part of the Finborough Hall Estate. The hall, built in 1795, has a big bow window and a colonnade of six Tuscan columns around it. Inside is an underground tunnel which leads from the kitchen into the gardens; it was reputedly built by a 19th century squire who wanted his servants hidden from view when they crossed the lawns to reach the kitchen garden. It is now a co-ed boarding school.

The Pettiwood family built the village hall, and a namesake is responsible for the, shall we say, rather unusual church spire which was erected in memory of his wife. I am not sure what she would have made of it!

The village maintains other links with the past including the annual Bogman Race which is traditionally held every Easter

Monday. The original race took place between two teams of labourers, one from Finborough and one from Haughley, who had both been given the job of digging the fields at nearby Boyton Hall on the edge of the village down Coombes Lane. Neither side wanted to give up the chance of a job, so a race was held from the hall to the Chestnut House pub. Apparently it was a fairly chaotic scene. Now participants are made up of anyone who feels like throwing themselves into the scrum, although there is no digging involved today, just a race. The first team to get to the pub is rewarded with free beer.

GREAT & LITTLE GLEMHAM

—— Stone Cottage was once the home of the favourite mistress of the then lord of the manor. He had a special gate built in the redbrick perimeter wall of Glemham House, so that he could have direct access to her 'cottage' when the mood took him. Apparently her property grew in size as her influence over him increased, until it took on the appearance of a substantial Georgian property. I wonder why they stopped there? Presumably their ardour cooled.

Grey-brick Glemham House was built in 1814, has an Ionic porch on a side entrance, and grounds which were originally laid out by Humphry Repton, the Regency architect and designer. Poet George Crabbe lived at Glemham House until 1801, and seemed in a much better frame of mind than when he was in Aldeburgh. Maybe it had something to do with the fact that Glemham means 'happy home'?

His son George has given a nostalgic account of their family life here. On summer evenings, the poet would read aloud from a novel as he walked in the gardens, while his son ran about netting moths and butterflies, and catching glow-worms. All the while the nightingales were singing their little hearts out. Sounds bliss.

The A12 at Little Glemham sweeps around the grounds of red-brick Glemham Hall, giving a good view of its north side and tree-lined avenue. It dates from the Elizabethan period, and was altered by Suffolk MP, Dudley North, between 1712 and 1725. The Cobbolds own it now and regularly hold open days. Take advantage of one if you can, if only to wander around the lovely rose garden.

GREAT LIVERMERE

——— Meander along the footpaths to enjoy the true solitude of this, despite its name, tiny village between Bury and Thetford. Perhaps it is this feeling of seclusion which attracts the ghostly figures for which it is famous. One local resident has even been keeping a log of spirit movements. I am sure Montague Rhodes James would have approved.

The author and scholar, and arguably one of the best ghost writers of the last century famed for his powerful writing rather than blood curdling phraseology, was born here in 1865 and lived until 1909 in the old rectory while his father was rector of the thatched St Peter's church. The secluded rectory grounds and Suffolk scenery fuelled the young James' imagination and he was to draw on local folklore and ghostly sightings for his books *Ghost Stories of An Antiquary* and *Warning to the Curious*. A memorial stone inside St Peter's was unveiled on the sixtieth anniversary of his death by the Ghost Story Society.

The last man to be hanged in Bury St Edmunds, Arundel Coke, once owned Livermere Hall. Motivated by jealousy, Coke tried to have his brother-in-law, Thomas Crisp, assassinated. But the plot failed as the murderer was half-cut and failed to deliver the fatal blow. Crisp put up a good fight, even cutting off the assassin's nose with a meat cleaver. Coke was hanged in 1721 as a result, and buried in Little Livermere church. It burned down in the 1920s.

The oldest gravestone in the churchyard, standing by the main door, is that of William Sakings, 'Forkner' (falconer) to three kings – James I, Charles I and Charles II – who died in 1689. He bred falcons in the thatched cottage next to the village green where the perches could be seen by passers-by. The birds were tagged with silver rings, one of which was found by a metal detector at Little Livermere.

GREAT SAXHAM

——— The next time you use nutmeg in cooking think of this village. John Eldred, a Turkey merchant, whose tomb and bust can be seen near the altar of St Andrew's, which also has some fine painted glass from France, built a manor house here known as Nutmeg Hall, having introduced the spice into England after his travels to Syria, Arabia and Egypt.

The hall burned down in 1779, but a new hall rose from the ashes. I managed to get quite a good look at the splendid white building, with its portico of four giant columns, standing in parkland, which can be reached through a kissing gate opposite the church. The original owner apparently asked Robert Adam to come up with a design, which was rejected. The landscape gardener Capability Brown managed to leave his imprint on the gardens including a Moorish Gothic temple and a serpentine.

Just nearby, through a gateway, past the lodge is a sign to Chevington. The ancient Chevington Way was the route from the Abbey at Bury to Chevington via Ickworth, before the village was emparked, and remained in use for many years after the transformation. Although closed by the then Earl of Bristol in 1814, it is still traceable for some of its length from Bury to the moated Abbot's Hall, to the north-west of the church.

The Earl closed the Way because he didn't like it wending its way through his park. The New Road that skirts the Ickworth estate was built by him, to compensate. Not as good as the original perhaps, but still a pleasant alternative to the busy main road from Bury.

GREAT & LITTLE THURLOW

—— Perhaps it is the combination of absolute prettiness and continuity of the generations, which makes the Thurlows so special. The villages flank the upper reaches of the river Stour some eight miles from Newmarket, and have a distinctly timeless quality, dominated as they are by the Thurlow estate, part of the Vestey family empire.

The estate owns 17,000 acres of surrounding countryside, houses about 90 pensioners and employs over 100 people. A number of retired estate workers or their widows are allowed to stay on in their tithed houses. As a result the appearance and vitality of both villages is unaffected by the pressures of the 21st century.

The Thurlows were known as Tritlawe and Tridlauva, thought to mean famous tumulus mound or assembly hill, and a possible reference to one of the many moated sites in and around the villages. Charles Foster Ryder bought the titles to both manors over a century ago; his daughter Sue spent her childhood in the area before gaining worldwide recognition for her international charity work.

In her book *The Forgotten Corner – A History of Thurlow*, Iris Eley lists a host of fondly remembered local characters. Tommy Smith the barber who would nip down to the pub for a swift half between customers and Millie Talbot, white witch, bee-swarmer and village midwife who kept a pet jackdaw on a string in her garden. During the Second World War tanks thundered down the main street which had become a temporary home to the London Irish Rifles with Bren gun carriers and more soldiers billeted at Little Thurlow Hall.

Tanks must have looked incongruous against the Jacobean school and almshouses founded by Sir Stephen Soame (1544-1619), and not an obvious subject for a sculpture. Little Thurlow church has a bronze of St Edmund by the late Dame Elizabeth Frink whose family lived in the area for a number of years.

GREAT WALDINGFIELD

Prose psalms set to rhyming couplets doesn't sound like a winning formula, but then who am I to say. John Hopkins and Thomas Sternhold certainly hit the big time when, under orders from Elizabeth I, they wrote a prayer book for the Church of England which was then applied to popular folk melodies, and French or Swiss hymn tunes, such as *All People That On Earth Do Dwell*. Their 1562 publication was the most popular book in England, after the Bible, for more than three centuries.

Hopkins is buried in the church, which has splendid monuments to the Kedington family, former lords of the manor. Ironically his name does not appear on the official list of rectors due to a combination of the fact that he missed his induction ceremony, and a clerical error. The name of his stand-in, John Cheetham, was entered instead.

St Lawrence's was partly restored in 1827 and again in 1869 when the chancel was rebuilt. The Reverend Bailey took a trip to the Holy Lands that year and brought back marble from Rome and granite from Mount Sinai, which were made into a mosaic which can be seen in the chancel. The alabaster cross is made from a fragment of a temple near the Sphinx in Egypt.

A footpath to the left of the church takes you to Little Waldingfield, a mile away, and on to Holbrook Hall once held by the Appletons. They built the almshouses in the churchyard and Samuel emigrated to America in 1636 to join his friend John Winthrop and found the colony of Massachusetts.

GROTON

Groton has a rich and varied wildlife population even if the numbers of humankind are comparatively few. The 50 acre Groton Wood is more than 400 years old and has a section that could be classified as from the first ages; a living link with the ancient wildwood which once blanketed Suffolk.

The Stars and Stripes flutters next to the Union Jack here. Groton has become a shrine for historically-minded Americans over the years and the famous broadcaster Alistair Cooke chose the village to embark on his noted 'History of America' series in the 1970s. Many place names familiar to East Anglia can be found on the East Coast of the USA today. And all because of the Winthrops.

Back in 1629 England was going through a turbulent time. Charles I was becoming increasingly unpopular as King and some feared he had Catholic sympathies. A group of like-minded men looked overseas to America where they had visions of founding a new colony based on Puritan values. The ringleader was John Winthrop. John was born in Edwardstone, but he lived with his family in Groton, and the story goes that while he was sitting under the village mulberry tree, he got the idea to head for the New World.

In April 1630 he set forth from the Isle of Wight on the 'Great Migration' with 17 ships and 1,000 emigrants bound for the Americas, carrying with him a charter from Charles I granting him powers of self-government. After a ten week crossing, they landed on a wild and desolate coast. John founded the city of Boston, where he is buried in King's Chapel, and became the first Governor of Massachusetts (1630-49). He has been described as 'the Father of New England'. The US wing of the Winthrops has established a trust, which provides funds for the church. John Winthrop XI was at the 350th anniversary celebrations in 1999. He got here in seven hours; rather less than the two and a half months it took his famous ancestor to reach the Americas.

GRUNDISBURGH

Grundisburgh has all the features of a classic Suffolk village – the green, the church, the pub and Victorian school. The red brick tower of St Mary's church, just across the river Fynn, had to be rebuilt in 1751 when the original flint tower fell down.

Inside, angels look down benignly from the splendid double hammerbeam roof, surely one of the most beautiful in Suffolk.

There is also a parapet with shields in the battlements and an inscription referring to Thomas Walle, a member of the London Salters' Club, and his wife Alice, daughter of Langston, master cook to Henry VII. The Walles are not recorded taking their culinary skills to Grundisburgh Hall, which dates from c.1500, with 19th century additions (the hall is down from the church, past Pound Corner, towards Culpho).

Sir John Wingfield owned it when it was 'Sigers', and the Blois family followed in the late 1500s when, as for villagers all over Suffolk, life was a struggle to survive against the odds. The Blois had no such trouble keeping their financial heads above water, and went on to achieve great wealth through the commercial success of their sugar-refining plant in Ipswich. The hall was bought by the Gurdon family at the end of the 18th century and one Robert Gurdon, Member of Parliament, chose the name Cranworth on his elevation to the peerage in 1899, after the Norfolk village where he lived. The village sign of cast panels and wrought iron work, displays three golden leopards' heads and is dedicated to the 2nd Baron Cranworth. A gentle reminder, lest we forget, that the family still owns the large village green.

The garden at Thatched Lodge is bordered by the grounds of Finndale House, the former home of George Lyttleton, father of jazz musician Humphrey. George's published letters to a former pupil talk of life in the village after the war, including references to the usual spats between neighbours and how there were not enough diversions to relieve the tedium of village life. Was it ever thus?

HADLEIGH

—— I have always advocated heading for the river to get a good overview of somewhere. The Riverside Walk, a half mile footpath beside the river Brett, takes you through marshes and woodland; the church spire and Deanery Tower popping into view on the opposite bank. Broom Hill nature reserve to the right, is accessible by several footpaths. Nearby Toppesfield Bridge has been called 'the one massive medieval bridge still in use in Suffolk', although it was widened in the 16th century, and was an important route for the town's medieval trade in wool.

The Deanery Tower of 1495 (known locally as Pykenham's Tower) was built by Archdeacon William Pykenham as the gate-house to his palace. Rising to six storeys, with embattled turrets, it was apparently the scene of the 'Hadleigh Conference' out of which developed, in 1833, the 'Oxford Movement', which aimed to restore Roman Catholic ideals to the Anglican Church.

Near the church, the timber-framed guildhall is testament to when Hadleigh was a leading cloth town in the 15th and 16th centuries. So successful were the enterprising Suffolk merchants and artisans in home-made cloth, that this commodity soon replaced wool as England's greatest export; helped in no small measure by the Flemish craftsmen who established their own communities in the area during the 14th century. The woollens were made in centres like Bury and Ipswich, and then processed in Hadleigh.

The principal Suffolk woollens were known by their colours – such as blue and azure – and by their quality, the cheapest being kerseys and straits and the most costly, the broadcloths.

HALESWORTH

—— The fortunes of this little market town were transformed when the river Blyth was made navigable in 1756 leading to an increase in the trade of the town's maltsters and brewers. Two members of the brewing family, William and Joseph Hooker, left Halesworth to become international botanists and, latterly, directors of Kew Gardens. Sir William lived in the Brewery House from 1809 to 1821, where son Joseph Dalton Hooker was born in 1817. He co-produced a vast work, *Genera Plantarum*, describing 7,569 varieties and 97,000 species of seed-bearing plants. His wife was called, enchantingly, Hyacinth.

Another prominent family here throughout the 16th to 18th centuries was the Bedingfields; Sir Henry was Lord Chief Justice under Charles II and Sir Robert was Lord Mayor of London in 1707. They lived at Gothic House from 1540.

The railway station has been returned to its Victorian splendour and now houses the town's museum, which includes the unique swing gates, each weighing eight tonnes, which were installed in 1888 when the main road between the town and Bungay passed right through the station. The Halesworth to Southwold Railway operated from 1879 to 1929 and its journey along the Blyth valley was one of the most picturesque in the region. There is evidence of the line over 70 years after it closed, such as the original footbridge across the Blyth between Walberswick and Southwold, and the cutting across Southwold Common. For more information, it is worth consulting *The Railway* by Eric Tonks and Peter Punchard.

HARTEST

—— You can find this jewel on a steep cleft of the river Stour about seven miles north of Sudbury. The green is large and handsome and nearly all the houses surrounding it are eye-catching. Like the Boxted and Hartest Club of 1888, or the late-Georgian stuccoed chapel with round-headed windows on the east side of the green, and the cluster of cute pink and green washed cottages.

Hartest was first mentioned in a grant of estates to Aelsi, Abbot of Ely Abbey, and it may have been about the period of his ministry (c. AD 981-1020) when a church was first established here. Perhaps the location was near to the manor hall, at the rear of what is now the Crown Inn, and was the Bishop's Palace in later years. It became known as the Crown from the mid 1700s and is well worth a look inside.

The church of All Saints has some interesting features, including a Jacobean pulpit and an original 16th century north porch door. The font hasn't had such a long life. During the Civil War, churchwarden Ambrose Dister of Peace Farm pulled it down, claiming pressure from the Earl of Manchester's soldiers who were said to be close by. Feelings ran high during this bloody period of English history, with both Roundheads and Royalists among the church congregation. More upheaval followed in 1650 when the church tower collapsed into the nave. Thomas Moore from East Bergholt agreed to 'bild the stepell up ten foote above the church', but needed an estimated £1,240 to complete the job. A request to raise the funds was made in a petition to Parliament. Perhaps a vain hope as the locals were 'exceeding poore'.

The glacial stone standing alongside the parish pump is said to have been dragged here from Somerton, as some form of celebration in the late 17th century, for the ending of the War of the Spanish Succession in the Caribbean. It was the focus of more jollity in 1789 when Mad King George recovered from one of his insane moments. Perhaps there was some quiet reflection here when former hostage, and now Hartest resident, Terry Waite was released from captivity in the mid 1990s.

HAUGHLEY

——— After the Normans arrived, a motte and bailey castle was built at the northern end of the village. It had to be a mainly wooden one of course, in this place known as 'haw-wood'. At the time, the castle was one of the most important in East Anglia; until the Earl of Leicester and his band of Flemish mercenaries set it alight in 1173. The timber turned to ash, but the earthwork still looks impressive, with a towering cedar marking the site of the keep. Part of the original moat is now a duck pond; further evidence can be seen in the churchyard.

After the destruction of the castle the Honour, or feudal Liberty, of Haughley, began to decline in significance although it was seen as important enough to be awarded to Charles Brandon, Duke of Suffolk, in Tudor times. The Parish was appropriated to the Abbot of Hales Abbey, Gloucestershire, who was ordered to erect a gallows in the field known as 'Luberlow'. A farmer was allowed to use the field as long as he supplied a ladder for the gallows.

Thirty leather buckets from 1725 hang from the rafters of St Mary's church. They were placed here as a fire precaution in bygone days (as so many Suffolk halls and manor houses have been lost to fire over the centuries, it was probably eminently sensible). The Jacobean 'E' plan manor house built by the Sulyard family in 1620 is a feature of Haughley Park and the gardens, woods and parkland are open to the public for limited days during the summer season.

The Lord of the Manor, Jeffery Bowden, proudly displays his coat of arms with golden bows and crossed swords set on a blue background, from a pole on the chimney of his listed Haughley House. He has traced his family back to the 17th century, and in one respect is merely following tradition; as hoisting your arms this way dates back to medieval times.

HAVERHILL

Although the town was one of the county's major cloth-makers in the 14th century because of its proximity to wool centres like Clare, it doesn't have too much to show of this golden period in its history. A great fire in 1665 all but destroyed Haverhill, but the arrival of silk weavers from Spitalfields triggered an economic upturn and the cottages in Weavers' Row were a hive of industry producing drabbet and silk.

In the late 1600s, the town became embroiled in the bitter religious strife that was dividing the kingdom. James I wanted peace with Spain to avoid expensive foreign wars, but the Puritans of England were prospering and pushed for an end to the Spanish monopoly of trade with the Americas. James resisted and to add fuel to the fire he allowed certain games to be played on a Sunday. For the likes of Haverhill Puritan Nathaniel Ward, this was the thin end of the wedge.

Nathaniel emigrated to Massachusetts and renamed the small community of Agarram as Ipswich (there is also a town in the US called Haverhill). He then wrote what has been described as the 'first humorous book written in America', *The Simple Cobbler of Aggawam*, in 1647 which includes such nuggets as: 'The Body beares the head, the head the Crown; If both beare not alike then one will down'. The Americans still rate him; he has his own web site.

To my knowledge Henry VIII's fourth wife hasn't got her own page on the internet. At the southern end of the town in Hamlet Road, a timber and brick building, now offices but still called 'Anne of Cleves House', was built in 1540 as part of her divorce settlement from the King (if you would like to know more, the history museum in the Gothic Town Hall in the High Street can help).

HELMINGHAM

You can learn a lot from reading the church visitors' book. The comments in this one range from 'somewhat unusual', to 'very quaint'. Certainly the marble tombs of the Tollemaches in St Mary's church are impressive by anyone's standards, particularly the one of John, 1st Baron Tollemache. Also that of General Thomas Tollemache who fought gallantly under William III in the wars with France; which, when they finally ended in

1713, established Britain's supremacy in Europe.

One of the best views of the stunning Tudor hall, with ornate chimneys, is right out of the church, through the gate and over the causeway between two rectangular fishponds and the 16th century obelisk. Its beauty is then perfectly reflected in the lake. The half-timbered hall, built around an inner court, is fully moated with a functioning cast-iron drawbridge. John Nash, of Brighton Royal Pavilion fame, added most of the south front with its finials, mullions and battlements, in the 18th century. The other moat surrounds the grand formal walled garden to one side, tended for 20 years by Lady Tollemache. You can catch her tips on a perfect herbaceous border when the gardens are open for part of the week in the summer.

I was told that during Christmas in 1900, the then Lady Tollemache used to provide broth for poor estate families. Her speciality was venison soup – not surprising with so many deer around – which would be distributed from a huge copper saucepan. It was known as 'buck-soup'.

Herds of fallow and red deer grazed contentedly amid the 400 acres of ancient parkland when I stopped by; a scene that can't have altered that much since the hall was built in 1485 by John Tollemache, on his marriage to Elizabeth Joyce from Helmingham. He moved the principal family seat here from Bentley and 18 generations of Tollemaches have lived here. The name comes from 'Talemache', meaning 'Keeper of the Seal', a post held by the family under Henry I, but the family is perhaps best known today for their connections with the brewery Tolly Cobbold.

HEMINGSTONE

—— Need an excuse for a refreshing walk among rolling countryside? Come here, and take in some fine architecture in the process. The Catholic Cantrells were the leading family in the 16th and 17th centuries before emigrating (or being driven out for their religious views) to the USA. To avoid punishment for refusing to attend the Protestant services of the Reformed Church, Ralph Cantrell built a vestry in St Gregory's; named after the Pope who sent the first Christian mission to Canterbury in AD 597. This was his personal chapel, 'Ralph's Hole', and deliberately had no view of the altar.

The massive iron door at the base of the church tower steps

acted as a safe when village valuables needed to be hidden away from sticky fingers. Perhaps the Cantrells stored their trinkets here when they lived at Stonewall Farm, originally Stone Hall, an early 14th century timber-framed building of a type known as Wealden. It has a central, open hall flanked by two-storey bays which jetty forwards, and a single roof which covers the whole, producing an overhang in front (the house is at the junction of the B1078 and the Gosbeck-Henley road).

Across the valley from the church is the red-bricked, Dutch-gabled Hemingstone Hall. The interior contains a number of fine rooms and large open fireplaces, with some nice contemporary input from the current owners, who have been restoring the hall, Forth-bridge like, since they moved in eight years ago. I was lucky enough to have a nose inside as part of the county's 'Invitation to View' scheme. There is some confusion as to when the hall was built exactly. The owners think 16th century with later additions; others believe later. The grounds, like the house, are Grade I listed and were laid out with some help from the designer Lanning Roper. As the outside is so lovely you almost don't need to step inside to appreciate its full beauty. Note the porch is not quite in the middle; country builders could get away with not being altogether symmetrical.

HENGRAVE

—— Happily, it is still possible to drive through the deep south Breckland woodland, skirt around the banks of the river Lark, and come upon the Tudor splendour of Hengrave Hall. Most of Suffolk's great houses were built of brick, or timber frame with wattle and daub, or lath and plaster. Hengrave is part white brick from the brickfields of Bury Abbey, and part stone, and is surely one of the most impressive houses of the later years of King Henry VIII (it is now a Christian retreat; tours by appointment).

The hall was built by London merchant Sir Thomas Kytson, from 1525 to 1538, although between 1524 and 1540 has been suggested as the more accurate date. It has turrets crowned with tiaras, and the piece de resistance is the heraldic bay window above the entrance, which is similar to those at Windsor Castle.

Queen Mary Tudor and Elizabeth I brought their courts here. They stayed in the Queen's Chamber (not at the same time of course) at the top of the great stairs, and perhaps worshipped in the chapel where there is a stained-glass window (c.1525) representing scenes from Genesis and the Life of Christ.

John Wilbye, one of England's greatest madrigalists, whose love songs include *Adieu Sweet Amaryllis*, and *Draw on, Sweet Night*, was resident musician at the hall for 30 years as Lady Kytson's Chief of the Minstrels. The room named after him overlooks the church, which is awash with monuments to Kytson as well as one to Thomas Gage Craufurd who fell at Waterloo. The Gages once lived at the hall. Sir William Gage cultivated the Gage plum (greengage) from France.

HERRINGFLEET

—— Towards the end of the 10th century, a Viking family arrived in their 70 foot long, 16 foot broad boats, looked around and thought: 'this will do nicely'. The possible landing point was at Marsh Lane, in front of the church. The round tower might have been a look-out, and weapons' store. Theories abound that it was also the local treasury. During the Second World War, Fritton Lake (Fridetuan, the Place of Freya, a Scandinavian goddess) was an army tank training centre. Some say there is a tank rotting away at the bottom of the lake.

It is a Dutchman we have to thank, indirectly, for the mill. Cornelius Vermuyden introduced the Dutch drainage mills into this country around 1620. The Herringfleet Marsh Mill, built around two centuries after, is the last survivor of the old-style Broadland windpump with cloth-spread sails and a boat-shaped cap turned manually by a tailpole and winch.

Many a wherry would have sailed past the mill in the late 19th and early 20th centuries. The huge black sails could be controlled by one rope, and only one man and a boy, often referred to as 'gypsy watermen', were needed to navigate the barge through the shallow waters of the Broads and under numerous low bridges (a stone bridge built around 1496 is depicted in a painting by Hobart in Loddon church). By 1850 there was keen competition between the wherry traffic on the river, and the new network of railways, for conveying heavy freight.

Henry Mussenden Leathes, commended for his role in Waterloo, once lived at Herringfleet Hall. After the great battle he moved to Lowestoft, with no lingering malice against the French. Quite the opposite. He showed such compassion for the Gallic fishermen, including turning his home over as a hospital

The Herringfleet Marsh Mill and wherry.

for them, that he was rewarded with a medal from the Emperor Napoleon III. On his way back to England, he stopped off at Cologne to do a spot of shopping, and purchased some painted glass, which can be seen in the east window of the church.

🌿 HEVENINGHAM

—— Pronounced 'Henningam', it's dominated by what some have called the grandest Georgian mansion in the county, Heveningham Hall, of which more later. Heveningham House, also Georgian, might not hold a candle to the hall, but it strikes quite a pose on the main route into the village and was said to have been the model for Nash's terraces in London's Regent's Park.

It is also a good starting point for exploring the lovely hamlet of cottages grouped together behind the church; cottages with decorative plasterwork, or pargeting, dating back centuries. The village pump and well are still there with a sign warning you not to drink the water unless you boil it first. Or freeze it?

In the grounds of the hall is a thatched ice house with the roof peeping through the ground and sheep happily munching away around it, built so the aristocracy could enjoy the benefits of cool food and drink throughout the year. The ice probably came over from Norway, chopped out of the fjords and shipped over to Ipswich.

Sir Robert Taylor designed the hall in 1778 for Sir Gerard Vanneck (van Neck) who had inherited the estate from his father, a Dutch merchant who moved to England in 1720. The exterior of this Palladian hall was designed in Classic style with central Corinthian columns and symmetrical pedimented wings. The park is being landscaped, over 200 years after it was originally laid out by Capability Brown in 1781. There is a lovely view of the hall as you come over the brow of the hill and as parking is almost impossible, so you have to just take your chance, stopping where you can and walking along one of the public footpaths that skirt the river and take you almost to the front door.

The Vannecks lived here for nearly 200 years. Since they left the hall has changed ownership many times. In the past, it has been open to the public on selected days during the summer. Watch the press for details, as they say.

HITCHAM

────── John Henslow became pastor in the first year of the reign of Queen Victoria, whose children he would later tutor. In 1837, life in the village wouldn't have prepared him for court life. It was described as: 'where the inhabitants were far below the average scale of the peasant class in England'.

The farmers were certainly too conservative for Henslow's tastes when it came to combating crop diseases, so he set about involving them in his experiments based on coprolite, which he had found in the cliffs of Felixstowe during a family holiday. John recognised that coprolites contained a high percentage of lime, which he thought would make a good fertiliser. From such humble beginnings the Fisons chemical company began. A small back alley close to the Ipswich docks, Coprolite Street, was where the fertiliser was prepared.

But botany was his first and main love. He had a flair for collecting insects and fossils, and while a schoolboy was invited to catalogue the British Museum's growing Natural History Collections. He went up to Cambridge in 1827, becoming Regius Professor of Botany, and would hold regular soirees for the great and the good in the world of science. A diffident undergraduate called Charles Darwin came along to one, and when in 1831

Henslow was asked to recommend a naturalist to join HMS *Beagle* for its scientific survey of South American waters, he suggested Darwin. *The Origin of Species by Means of Natural Selection* was the result. Darwin visited Henslow at Hitcham and you can just picture them sitting on one of the benches under the trees in the churchyard, perhaps sharing a beverage or two.

Fellow pastor John Staverton Mathews (1801–37) had Hitcham Rectory, now Hitcham House, rebuilt in its present form, making it a fitting seat for a wealthy squire-parson. He was popular in the village for his generosity and used to open the annual Tithe Feast with a popular song: 'He that drinks strong beer and goes to bed quite mellow, lives as he ought to live and dies a hearty fellow'. Cheers!

HOLBROOK

—— The footpath from Stutton church to Lower Holbrook skirts the Royal Hospital School standing proud on the banks of the river Stour on the Shotley Peninsula, and in my opinion offers the most dramatic view of this wonderful building with its prominent tower rising over the playing fields like a guardian angel. The school was founded in 1821 at Greenwich, but the 860 acre estate was moved to Holbrook in 1933. It was originally dedicated to training young lads in the Naval style; now it is co-ed.

England's greatest naval commander, Horatio Nelson, was a natural at sea and survived on little formal education although he was known for his mastery of ancient languages, like Greek. But he made no attempt to hide his Norfolk accent and as he lay dying from a musket wound, he ordered his Flag Captain Hardy: 'Do you anchor, Hardy'.

Holbrook author Robert Malster knows all about peculiar ways of speaking, recorded in his book *The Mardler's Companion, A Dictionary of East Anglian Dialect*. Much of the dialect has survived since the time of Chaucer and has Germanic or Danish influences. There are differences running through the county from east to west, and along the Waveney valley, where people speak neither Norfolk nor Suffolk, but their own 'speak'. But what unites Suffolk is the double negative – 'I hun't got nought.'

I wonder what the Suffolk term for an embalmed head might be? One was found in 1863 in the chancel of All Saints' church, where the splendid marble tomb of Judge Clench lies in the corner. It was he who on the 25th March 1586 sentenced Margaret Clitheroe to death by crushing, in York. During the reign of Henry VIII, it was an offence to be a practising Catholic, yet Margaret, a devout Catholic, would hold Mass in her home and hide priests to save them from capture. She was crushed beneath an 800 lb weight, taking 15 minutes to die. I am sure she must have felt like uttering a few choice words.

HOMERSFIELD

The two claims to fame here are a bat and a bridge. Homersfield is on the edge of no-man's-land, incorporating some of Suffolk's more remote villages: the four Ilketshalls, and the seven South Elmhams, one of which, St Mary's, is more commonly known as Homersfield.

There has been a crossing here since ancient times as the figure of a Roman soldier standing guard on the bridge would suggest. The single-span iron bridge (by the Black Swan pub) was erected here by the Adair family of Flixton Hall in 1870, and was the first concrete and cast-iron bridge of its type in the country. It carried traffic through the village until the 1970s and is now a footbridge, where you can stop and watch kingfishers swooping down to the water, catching the fish before the men in waders do. And if you are very lucky, the pipistrelle bat, the smallest of these British flying mammals, might interrupt his nocturnals and put in an appearance. This is one of the few places he frequents, apparently.

As you come into the village, Barnfield Cottages, a semi-circle of thatched cottages built to provide retirement homes for workers on the nearby Flixton Estate, is a lovely sight. One Homersfield resident, Sir Nicholas Hare, could have enjoyed his twilight years in one of these after a busy and illustrious career as Master of the Rolls in 1553, and Lord Chancellor in 1555.

Church Wood next to St Mary's was bought by the village in 1998, with a little help from the European Regional Development Fund. A bridleway, part of the Angles Way long distance path, runs along the eastern boundary. Old oaks and large wych elms can be found here, and during the Second World War, the oaks were felled to provide timbers for mine-sweepers being built at Lowestoft. Down the bridlepath and left to the fishing lake, is the site of such finds as a woolly mammoth tusk and Roman pottery kilns.

HONINGTON

—— The parish church, Bloomfield's house, the post office and the new burial ground where the rectory once stood, are grouped in a huddle. The post office has fine wooden doors rescued from the old rectory after it burned down in 1783. It holds the key to the church which has a plaque, erected in 1916 at the 150th anniversary of the birth of the little known ploughman-poet, Robert Bloomfield.

A wattle and daub house by the church, now divided into two, was where Robert, the youngest of six children, was born. His mother Elizabeth was the village schoolmistress, a formidable lady by all accounts. She is credited with saving the doors after the rectory fire began to threaten her nearby property. She is said to have fled to a field, clutching the deeds to her house and the family clock. Not before raising the alarm presumably.

Robert's first job was on his uncle's farm at nearby Sapiston and it was undoubtedly his love of rural life that was to kick-start his poetry. First published in 1800, *The Farmer's Boy* sold 26,000 copies in less than three years and has been translated into several languages. Despite tragedy and ill health, Robert continued to write, including *Rural Tales* and *The Banks of Wye*. In true artistic fashion, he died in poverty at the age of 57.

> 'Strange to the world he wore a bashful look,
> The Fields his study, Nature was his book'
> – *'Farmer's Boy' (Spring)*

No one visiting Honington can miss the nearby RAF airfield. The old airfield chapel was transferred to its present site in Sapiston in 1946 by the Americans, as a mark of their appreciation of the friendship given to them by the local people during the conflict. It is now the village hall.

HORHAM

—— You could say this is a village to make music by. Aldeburgh Festival founder Benjamin Britten came here to compose, among other works, *The Little Sweep* (about Iken Hall) away from Aldeburgh, which at the time was blocking his creative flow. He composed in a purpose-built room at the bottom of his garden, overlooking Horham fields, and near the

Baptist chapel. By all accounts he kept himself very much to himself.

The other man of music to spend time here was Glenn Miller who visited Horham airbase to celebrate the airfield's 200th mission during the Second World War. There is an impressive 1981 American War Memorial near the church dedicated 'In memory of the men of the 95th Bombardment Group who served at Horham Airfield 1943-45'. There were up to 400 Yanks stationed here during the war, to the delight of local pubs like the Green Dragon, which saw beer sales take off. The Americans didn't mind the 'warm' beer it seems. They even helped to restore the eight bells in the church; the oldest set in the world.

Vikings settled here with King Canute; today the B1117 road from Eye to Halesworth, which cuts through the parish, bends to go round the churchyard. A short distance along the road to the south-east of the church is the Old Post Office (Ancient House), which is a lovely 16th century house, built of Tudor bricks and believed to stand on the site of a 12th century Lady Chapel. David Spall, who runs the new post office next door to Ancient House, where he lives and which he has been restoring, told me the property has a moat underneath which leads to a tithe barn, and is in all probability part of a ten acre estate owned by the Jernegan family, one time lords of the manor. So has he come upon any ghosts? 'If there are any, they took all the money!', he joked.

Thorpe Hall, one mile north of the village, is a fine brick house (c.1560) designed in the style of a hunting-lodge or summerhouse with rather splendid chimney stacks with star tops. All the windows are brick with mullions and pediments, rendered to simulate stonework.

HOXNE

—— Some villages ooze history from every pore, metaphorically speaking, and Hoxne is one of them. Or should that read pre-history? Three thousand years ago Stone Age men roamed the lakeside on the edge of the village on the road to Eye, shaping and sharpening their flints and axes while their oxen and deer grazed nearby. Thousands of years later, the legendary King Edmund the Martyr was to put Hoxne on the map forever.

There are a number of different versions as to how and where Edmund met his death but one of the most likely places is Hoxne. The story goes that in AD 870 Edmund was captured by the

King Edmund hiding under the Goldbrook bridge, from a relief sculpture on the wall of the village hall.

Danes at a 'vill' called Heglisdune, and on refusing to renounce Christianity, was tied to a tree and slain by a volley of arrows until: 'his body resemble an urchin fulfilled with sprigges thicke'. Edmund's head was then severed and thrown into the wood where it was supposed to have been guarded by a wolf. The King was buried where he fell until his body was moved to what is now Bury St Edmunds, 30 years later.

On the outskirts of the village, standing alone in open cornfields, is a stone cross marking the spot where in 1848, an oak tree fell and shattered into pieces, revealing an arrow head embedded in the ancient trunk. (Is this where Edmund met his untimely death?) From here, approaching the village, you cross Goldbrook bridge where legend has it that after a bloody battle, Edmund hid before being spotted by newly weds who saw the reflection of his gold spurs in the water, and reported his whereabouts to the Danes. Edmund put a curse on the bridge that even today is an unpopular crossing point for brides. The story is depicted on a circular plaque on the village hall.

IKEN

In my view, the best way to see this tiny promontory overlooking the Alde is by boat. Dropping anchor in the narrow channel in front of St Botolph's church is a truly wonderful way to spend a relaxing, sunny afternoon. As the highlights of this tiny community are conveniently packed into a small area by the church, leaving your car in Church Road and walking the short distance up to St Botolph's is a pretty good second.

According to documents the 'unwearied man of God looked about him everywhere 'til at last he found by the mercy of God such a spot, Ikano, which was just the God-foresaken devil-possessed place he was in search of'. Botolph founded a Saxon monastery here around AD 654 when the area was known as Icanhoh. He must have marvelled at the dawn chorus of avocets and oyster-catchers, which probably interrupted his early morning prayers in summer and likewise he surely would have had difficulty with the mud-flats as the tide ebbed. Before the Second World War, shooting was free for all up to the high-water mark, as noted by *Suffolk Scene* author Julian Tennyson.

In 1977 a carved limestone cross shaft was found in the walls of the church. Its date would indicate that it was a memorial to St Botolph. Further excavations revealed Saxon pottery. As though maintaining the tradition, in the summer months there is a stall just outside the church positively groaning with locally-produced

Iken.

pots and plant holders. I often head here in search of ideas for birthday presents.

The only downside is running the gauntlet of rather ferocious-sounding dogs guarding the neighbouring grand Anchorage House with its superb Italianate garden cascading down to the river. Head inside St Botolph's for some peace and quiet and climb up to the parapet and absorb the view. You can see why it would have been a splendid vantage point to spot any invaders with malice on their mind coming up the river.

🍃 IPSWICH

——— There are hints of glories past here, including 16th and 17th century merchants' houses. Ancient House (Sparrowe's House) in the Buttermarket has wonderful bay windows and an overhanging first floor. The Sparrowes were a family of merchants and Robert commissioned the fine pargeting, in the 1660s, of birds, flowers and Neptune riding a sea horse. East Anglia is rich in pargeting not least because there has been little change here compared to other regions. Inside (now a kitchen store) reveals the wonderful old oak beams and studwork.

Thomas Wolsey was born in nearby Silent Street in 1472. Son of an Ipswich butcher, he rose to be Henry VIII's Lord Chancellor, and in 1528 he founded the Cardinal College of St Mary in his home town as a rival to Eton and Winchester. But after falling out with Henry in 1529, the project foundered and all that remains of his dream is Wolsey's Gate in College Street on the edge of the docks. There are plans to restore the modest redbrick gate, standing, forlornly, among gleaming new apartments. The Docks were once known as 'The London Shipyard', as most of the London merchants had their ships built here from the oak growing in the county's forests.

When I'm in a queue of traffic heading out of the town, I often sneak a left turn at the bus station to while away a few hours in Christchurch Mansion, a hive of history hidden away in a beautiful wooded and hilly park. It was built in 1548 on the site of the 12th century Holy Trinity Priory, and is bulging with Constables and Gainsboroughs. Constable often painted here; Gainsborough picked up his palette from 1752 to 1759, making a living from painting Ipswich notables. *Mr and Mrs Andrews* was his first masterpiece.

Gainsborough's house is no longer, but the half-timbered

Unitarian Meeting House in Friars Street, one of the earliest Nonconformist chapels in England, has stood the test of time. Daniel Defoe said of it: 'The interior is the best finished I have ever seen, London not excepted'. All the seats face inwards, symbolising the congregation pulling as one.

KEDINGTON

—— Some locals call it Kitten or Ketton, popular in times past. Certainly crossing the threshold of the church is like stepping back centuries. There is Roman work (was it a Romano-British cemetery?) under the floorboards of the pews. The main part of St Peter & St Paul, 'The Westminster of Suffolk', is 11th century with a low-pitched Tudor roof, a Georgian singing gallery and an unusually complete Jacobean three-decker pulpit. The great Protestant preacher, Samuel Fairclough, might have used it; complete with sermon timer so no one nodded off.

The sexes definitely were not allowed to mix in the Barnardiston pew, with separate compartments for men and women. Until the 18th century, Kedington was as good as owned by the Barnardistons who were the leading family of Suffolk Puritans, and here they all lie including Sir Nathaniel, onetime MP for Sudbury. He nearly lost out on a knighthood because of his Puritan ways but was knighted in Newmarket in 1618, the 23rd in the family.

He died in London and his body was brought back to Kedington in considerable style. The cortege was met 20 miles outside of the village and his funeral attended by thousands who had come to pay their respects to one so universally loved. Apparently he was a benevolent employer. Son Samuel marched on London where Queen Henrietta, looking out of the window, saw him and cried, 'See what a handsome round head is there,' and the name was adopted.

The Barnardiston mansion behind the church was pulled down around 1780. A knight is supposed to be buried under the row of elms along Church Walk. Maybe it is Thomas Barneston, listed as a knight in the subsidy returns of 1524. The attractive redbrick Queen Anne house, half a mile from the church, used to be the rectory.

On the edge of the village is the Risbridge Union Workhouse, opened in 1857 when it was the biggest building in the area housing a third of the population, approaching 1,000. For once, there are not any recorded complaints. On the contrary, although the exterior was typically forbidding, the residents seem to have not minded being confined within its walls.

KELSALE-CUM-CARLTON

In the early 1800s, Kelsale was a microcosm of Georgian life with no fewer than three butchers' shops. My house used to be one, and every time we redecorate the study, the old abattoir, bits of old sheep and pig make an appearance from under the plaster work.

Happily the heart hasn't been torn out of what is still essentially a 'neat village lying in the vale of a small rivulet', as described in an old directory. Walk down the main street and you can still get a sense of life once revolving around the farms and small holdings, and the weekly market, established since Domesday, held near the fine old Guildhall. The hall was part of the Order of St John, and run by a priest to provide shelter for monks and the poor, who were fed, watered, and even provided with a good burial and prayers said for their soul, if they joined the guild. No wonder many took up the offer on their death beds!

Drunks and criminals from as far away as Dunwich were banished to the dungeons (still evident today) below the old Georgian-style court house, Kelsale Court. According to folklore, on seeing the splendour of the building, local benefactor Samuel Clouting decided to erect his own pile close by. Years later, it became the Eight Bells pub, now a property developer's headquarters. The wrought-iron initials 'S' and 'C' are above the door.

Another architectural feast stands near the 11th century church of St Mary and St Peter on the hill immediately above the village. Kelsale old manor has a garden originally designed by famous landscape gardener Gertrude Jekyll (1843-1932), and apparently vineyards once thrived here in the 16th century; probably the first in Suffolk. From 1967 until the early 1980s, the new lord and lady of the manor tried their hands at a spot of wine producing. I managed to find a bottle of the 1981 vintage, which was surprisingly quaffable. The sort of wine to take on a picnic, or a walk in the fields around Carlton church where in spring with poppies swaying in the breeze, it doesn't take too many mental leaps to imagine yourself in northern France.

KERSEY

—— Despite all his travels, Ralph Hammond Innes never forsook Kersey and when he returned from London and crossed the Stour he was said to have felt: 'a sudden magic, the quintessential of an English landscape miraculously materialising before our eyes'. It is rather surprising that an adventure writer of bestsellers such as *Attack Alarm* and his final book, *Delta Collection*, lived in such a serene environment. Maybe it was the contrast that appealed to him. He died at his home in June 1998 after clocking up an impressive 84 years, a total of 34 books and sales exceeding 50 million copies world-wide.

Innes' stunning 16th century house stands behind enormous wrought iron gates, among wonderful landscaped gardens. His wife was gifted in the green fingers department, apparently. There are plans to erect a blue plaque to Innes. In the meantime the best way to find his former home is to approach from the church end, follow the main street for about 20 yards and his house is on the left before the ford. Innes pledged a substantial part of his £6.8m estate to the Association of Sea Training Organisations, to help children from under-privileged backgrounds learn to sail. The Kersey brook descends from Milden and flows through the bailey of Lindsey Castle, a moated mound now rather overgrown with brambles. Sadly not enough water for 'Swallows and Amazons' adventures.

The main street runs north/south down the side of a narrow valley to the Splash, a tributary to the river Brett, and up the other side to the pretty church at the top. There are several excellent, mainly Elizabethan, buildings along the way; notably Woodbine Cottage, Ye Olde River House, Denbigh House, and the Old Drift House. Even with Lavenham so close, Kersey has earned the title: 'the most beautiful village in south Suffolk'. Most of the houses have large windows on the first floor to give lots of light to weavers, when Kerseymere wool cloth or woolsey, was produced here. It gets a mention in Shakespeare's *Love's Labour's Lost* when the character Berowne vows in future to express his wooing in 'russet yeas and honest Kersey noes'.

KETTLEBURGH

—— Kettleburgh was once on the outer borders of the land ruled by the Iceni tribe under Queen Boudicca. Then came along a Viking called Ketyl who decided not to raid but to stay and call this village home.

Sir William Charles was granted the right to hold a market here in 1264, and a fair in 1291; it was he who laid the foundations for New Hall in 1261. The building was completed in the 16th century and has distinctive star-topped chimneys.

Going up to St Andrew's church is like going through someone's private garden. They don't object, apparently. Objections were made though to the behaviour of a farm labourer in 1879, who the worse for drink, was convicted by Framlingham magistrates for riotous and indecent behaviour at the church during a Sunday afternoon service. The story goes he sat in the gallery with his dog on his lap and urged the dog to: 'Speak to 'em lad' , which was the cue for the dog to exercise his vocal chords. Man and dog were ejected, and the service abandoned. He was fined £2.10s.0d. Better than being sent to prison, perhaps, which would have happened if the labourer had displayed such irreverent behaviour in a chapel.

White's Directory of Suffolk, 1844, records Samuel Hart, 'Herbalist and Poet' as living here. He advertised himself as 'Curer of bunions, scab heads, Rheumatism, Scrofula and various other complaints incidental to the human frame. Poems and Pieces composed and arranged on any occasion'. Some of the gravestones in the churchyard carry his verses (often illegible), such as for Hannah, wife of William Farthing, who died in 1854:

> Her last words when on her deathbed lie, she
> spoke plain and not bewilderin:
> She said dear husband I must die; Pray provide
> for my poor children.

KNODISHALL

—— Knodishall has the distinction of being called the 'ugliest village in Suffolk'. Some of you might challenge this with more horrible examples, but as the locals are rather proud of their claim to fame, who are we to question? In its defence, Knodishall is a parish, rather than village, with two main parts. At one time the parish included Buxlow, some two miles to the north-west, which had its own church.

The area is now called Knodishall Green, home to the splendid

Red House Farm, once known as Ghosts' Hole, and now Buxlow Manor, which has an Elizabethan 'E' plan, although the current Dutch gabled building was built in 1678. What remains of the old church, St Peter's, lies in a heap in the grounds. This, as you might have gathered, is the pretty bit of Knodishall. (Carry along here towards Kelsale, following the railway line, and you reach Knodishall gatehouse that has verges bursting with golden daffodils in the spring.)

The story goes that after the Black Death the village centre moved away from the church of St Lawrence to where it is now. The bubonic plague had already ravaged the population of Europe before reaching London in 1348 and spreading rapidly across the south of England. The burial of the dead aroused bitter feelings, as the Church insisted that only consecrated churchyards could be used. However, people were convinced that even beneath the ground bodies were sources of infection. So they moved away. St Lawrence's was substantially renovated following the sale of an 1851 painting, *Jacob and Rachel*, by William Dyce RA, in 1983. Other churches in Suffolk might wish they too could sell off the family silver during hard times.

The greens and common land in and around Knodishall are its main features, and 'Commoners' Rights' are still exercised on Knodishall Common. This is near the centre of the main village on the opposite side of the river Hundred, which runs into the Meare in Thorpeness en route to the sea, and has a tendency to burst its banks and flood local houses. In 1312 Knodishall held a Coldfair on one of its greens (known as Coldfair Green and widely held as the 'really ugly part'); for a while the fair was dropped, but was revived in 1988.

LAKENHEATH

In 1999, 160 graves, dating back 1,300 years, were found when work began on a new dormitory at the airbase. One contained the grave of an ancient warrior, his horse, his shield, sword and spear. His ribs and spine were removed intact and are now at the British Museum. Ancient warriors meeting the modern ones, you might say.

Lord Kitchener might have something to say about that. There is a marble memorial tablet to the Secretary of State for War ('Your Country Needs You') during the First World War, in the church. He drowned when HMS *Hampshire* went down in 1916. The London Society of East Anglians of which he was President erected the tablet. The Kitchener family lived in the village and a number of them are buried in the churchyard.

An ivy-covered dovehouse, by some farm buildings just as you come into the village, is the old parish church of St Peter at Eriswell. All that is left is two walls and a 15th century window. An early 18th century sketch shows a tower with a beacon on top, probably demolished (albeit partly) for the sake of its stones.

An Anglo-Saxon called Lak landed without the help of beacons at a hythe (landing spot) said to be a small quay, which has now become Mutford Green. Up until the last century, farming was the main occupation in the 11,000 acres, 3,000 of them warrens. Now the RAF base has taken charge and become, it seems, not only guardian of the air but of the treasure troves buried below.

LAXFIELD

No fewer than 48 of the thatched and timbered buildings have been scheduled as 'of historic and architectural interest', including the brick-nogged Guildhall of St Mary. The Guildhall was donated by the lord of the manor, in 1461, as a church house; it is now the local museum showing aspects of rural life over the past 100 years.

It's opposite the thatched King's Head (Low House) which has old photos lining the bar rooms, and where you can thump your empty glasses or flagons on the table and a wench will come and re-fill them. That's the theory anyway!

William Dowsing is thought to be from the Laxfield Dowsings, although there is no proof. 'By vertue of a pretended commission', he was made Parliamentary Visitor in 1643-4 and he, his deputy Edmund Glanfield of Gosbeck, and his band of destroyers set about a smashing campaign. His diary makes grim reading as with every entry you can almost hear the shattering of ancient coloured glass, or an angel falling from a hammerbeam roof. They didn't destroy much in the 14th century All Saints church. It had already suffered in the 16th century when Laxfield was a Puritan parish, so there was little left for the Puritans of Cromwell's time to do.

At the Baptist chapel (c.1808) there is a memorial stone to the shoemaker John Noyes who was burned at the stake in 1577 for his Puritan beliefs. It is said that on the day of his death everyone in the village put out their fires except for one. The constable and his assistant spotted a wisp of smoke coming from the chimney and broke down the door to get to the fire. One of those watching as Noyes was burned at the stake had his comments misinterpreted and ended up being put in the stocks and whipped around the market place the following Sunday.

LEISTON

—— It might not seem the hot-bed of communism now, but there was a time when workers' rights were top of the agenda here. The Garrett's engineering works, which once dominated the greater part of the town, pioneered the use of steam engines in farm machinery; as still exhibited at the Long Shop Museum. The Garretts were anti-unions; local artist and communist councillor, Paxton Chadwick from Manchester, took up the cudgels on behalf of the workers soon after his appointment as art teacher at Summerhill School in 1933. The Leiston United Front was formed and in 1946, Chadwick became the first Communist Council Chairman in the country. Around this time he moved back into his studio on the common.

Chadwick never painted Leiston Abbey, to the north of the town, to my knowledge, but it would have made a pretty picture. The abbey was founded by Sir Ranulf Glanville (see also Butley Priory), Lord Chief Justice, for Premonstratensian canons in 1182. The original building was moved inland to its present site in 1363 and still includes the church transept, a range of cloisters and a fine Tudor brick gatehouse. A music school is now housed here and recitals are held in the summer.

If you don't mind the reactors, I reckon the best beach around for a bracing walk is at Sizewell, where the fishing boats on the shore are as attractive as any in Aldeburgh. I often borrow a friend's dog for the walk south to Thorpeness, past old Sizewell Hall, with its steps leading down to the beach providing cover for what could have been a carriage stop. The hall is now a Christian Conference Centre but you can walk on the path alongside and dart behind the wall for a look. The folly here could well have been a lookout at one time.

The Kenton and Goode Hills Walks through the woodlands are part of Sizewell, offering a carpet of bluebells in the spring, white admiral and speckled wood butterflies among the rhododendrons in the summer and in autumn, colourful fungi. A guide is available at Sizewell Visitors' Centre.

LETHERINGHAM & HOO

—— Through farming country, over wide ditches, through gentle valleys and atop the willowy upper Deben you find Letheringham. A small Augustinian priory was founded here in 1194 as a cell of St Peter in Ipswich. Like many abbeys in the area, all that remains is the gatehouse, which is of 15th century brick. The Norman church of St Mary incorporates parts of the old priory (the church was originally the nave) and contains extremely good brasses to the Wingfield family. In the 16th century Margaret Wingfield married Thomas Seckford, father of Sir Thomas Seckford of Bealings and Woodbridge. Bookcases provide protection for valuable fragments of the Wingfield memorials.

The truncated St Mary's is almost lost in farmland. You need a four-wheel drive sometimes to get through to the church and the nerve to avoid running over a few cockerels if you follow the signed entrance. It is a lot easier to put on your wellies and stomp through the farm buildings. It is worth it. You also get a chance to pat the punches in the field next door.

Letheringham Hall, with its large weatherboard barn, is near the mill on the Letheringham-Easton road. The old watermill, set

Letheringham watermill.

in five acres of watermeadows, stopped work before the Second World War and most of the machinery has been removed. Recent restoration work has included the construction of a new wooden waterwheel, which can be seen turning on public open days. I can vouch it is wonderful in the spring when the grounds are covered with every imaginable spring flower.

The village of Hoo, one mile north-west of Letheringham, is possibly one of the smallest villages in Suffolk to have a village sign. Farming has always been the main pastime here and this, coupled with Hoo (meaning hill), led to the design for the sign which is of a horse ploughing on a hill. Which is funny, as it is flat as you enter Hoo, only inclining towards Letheringham where mud spattered roads can easily become dirt tracks.

LEVINGTON

—— On the estuary of the river Orwell, sailing boats and pleasure crafts swarm around the marina. In the past there were more sinister goings on. The notorious smuggler Margaret Catchpole operated from here and the Ship Inn, reputedly built from ships' timbers, was said to be a centre of her illegal goings-on.

Levington is also the birthplace of Admiral Edward Vernon, hero of the Battle of Portobello fought against the Spanish in Panama. Vernon was nicknamed 'Old Grog' as he always wore a grogram, or camel-hair coat. In 1740 he gave orders to dilute the sailors' rum ration and since then the mix has been called 'grog', hence it made the imbibers 'groggy'. The rum rations were withdrawn in 1970.

Sir Robert Hitcham, who bought Framlingham Castle from the Duke of Norfolk in 1635 for £14,000 was also born here, and was the force behind St Peter's broad brick-tower, completed in 1636, and the redbrick almshouses. There are a couple of other interesting buildings nearby including the Gothic-style Hill Cottage (c.1800) and the Levington Research Station, which was built by Birkin Haward in 1956. In the 18th century Edmund Edwards made the discovery that 'crag' (deposits of shelly sand) made an excellent fertiliser and, in 1940, Fison's bought Red House Farm and developed it into an experimental agricultural centre (see also Hitcham).

It would be nice to think it might have helped keep the greenfly off the roses. Levington was apparently the first village on the Orwell to have cultivated the rose.

LIDGATE

The Romans and a friend of Chaucer are not likely to have too much in common, but they are both linked to this tiny village, seemingly miles from nowhere, in some of Suffolk's finest countryside, yet only nine miles from civilisation. Well, Bury anyway.

The remains of a splendid Romano-British corridor-villa, with a main room and two side wings sub-divided into more than 20 rooms, was discovered on the outskirts of the village in the 1970s, and hopes are running high that funds will be available to uncover its true delights this century. A few years ago, an 89 year old resident was clearing out his cupboards when he found an old tin box that had been lying around for years. To his delight it held 20 coins, mainly from the reign of George III, but also including a Roman coin featuring the Emperor Ticitus who held the reins of power for just nine months in AD 275. A rare find indeed.

The church lies in the bailey of a former castle adapted by the Normans. It has brasses to John Lidgate, the celebrated 14th century poet-translator who wrote 150,000 lines of poetry and hung out with Geoffrey Chaucer. You can see some similarities in style in his Early English text:

> In May when Flora, the fressh(e) lusty quene,
> The soyle hath clad in grene, rede and white,
> And Phebus gan to shede his stremes shene,
> Amyd the Bole wyth al the bemes bryght.
> (from *A Complaynt of A Loveres Lyfe*)

Suffolk House, in the main street, is claimed to be his birthplace. It has a Tudor gable, once stepped, and over-sailing front, which is half weatherboarded. He was ordained priest in 1397, but apparently as a young boy, he tried to avoid going into church, preferring to count cherries instead.

LINDSEY

It probably gave its name to 'linsey-woolsey', a mixture of linen and wool, and was closely associated with the neighbouring village of Kersey where 'carsey', a coarse narrow cloth, was produced. A small river flows through the bailey of Lindsey Castle in the south of the parish. This was a motte and bailey structure, built at the same time as those at Offton and Milden, while arguments over who should succeed to the throne were raging between Matilda and King Stephen during the 'nineteen long winters' of his reign (1135–54). The castle covers some six acres and the river was probably used to fill its moats.

The building of these great defensive earthworks would have involved an enormous workforce; in a county which then probably amounted to less than 100,000 people. The mound is not immediately obvious as it is overgrown with trees. Local people call it Boar Hill. Nearby Elizabethan-style Castling's Hall has been in the hands of the Knyvets and then the Cloptons, one time owners of Kentwell Hall. Their memory lives on in the Clopton Chantry in Long Melford church which records no fewer than 55 of their tombs. One reads: 'bountiful and liberal and skilled and proficient in all the arts, famed for his gentle blood, William Clopton is confined in this narrow tomb, but all too straight for so great a friend of virtue'.

Castling's Hall is quite hard to find, lying between steeply hedged fields on the way to Groton. St James' is easier to locate as you enter the village from Kersey. The small medieval chapel was built in the early 13th century (the south wall is in its original state) to serve the adjacent Lindsey Castle, and as a 'chantry' where a priest would pray for the soul of the founder; a common medieval practice. In the mid 13th century, a member of a wealthy local family, Nestade Cockfield, is known to have instigated a tithe tax to pay for the chapel. Not a popular move.

LITTLE SAXHAM

—— Of Suffolk's 41 round towers, St Nicholas' is possibly the finest. Round towers are generally only found in East Anglia and nearly all date from Saxon or Norman times. Such round towers were erected mainly for defence, and it can be no coincidence that they are mostly near the coast, vulnerable to Danish raids. They are peculiar to this area because of the lack of freestone with which to make the quoins, or corners (The Round Tower Churches' Society, Crabbe Hall, Burnham Market, King's Lynn, Norfolk PE31 8EN).

The church vestry now houses the massive baroque monument to William, 1st Baron Crofts (d.1677) and his second wife

Elizabeth, by Abraham Storey and said to be his finest. Sir William ('Madcap') Crofts of Little Saxham Hall (now demolished) was the guardian of Charles II's natural son, Captain Crofts, later the ill-fated Duke of Monmouth. The Duke's ambitions to the throne came to a bloody end at Sedgemoor, Somerset, in 1685. He and his troops were slaughtered where they stood, in a boggy ditch, by government troops.

Charles would pay visits to the hall when he came to the Newmarket races, and Madcap had a special apartment built so that the King could entertain in private. On one visit in April 1670, the King attended a service with a lengthy sermon from George Seignior, a Fellow of Trinity College, Cambridge. Charles apparently warmed to the theme, and later had the sermon printed by His Majesty's special command (a copy is in the West Suffolk Record Office). Samuel Pepys recorded this visit to Saxham in his inimitable diary but some of the pages of his manuscript have been cut out; it seems to have been a scene of total debauchery! Pepys bequeathed his observations to Magdalene College, Cambridge.

LITTLE WENHAM

—— Little Wenham barely exists as a village, but standing in an isolated spot just to the north-west of Capel St Mary is a building that is one of the finest examples of 13th century housing – Little Wenham Hall and Castle.

To find it, follow the signs to the 13th century, Grade I listed, All Saints church, worth a look itself. Natural light through the leaded windows highlights the medieval religious paintings that still surround the altar and are just visible on the wall opposite the main door. The painted faces might have oxidised over the years so that they are now black, but the blue and red of the figures' robes have worn well. The church was declared redundant in 1976 but services are held there in the summer.

Standing atop the church steps offers a good view of the hall. On summer evenings, the castellated pale yellow walls are shown in their best hue. They are one of the earliest examples of home-made brick, with only the base of flint and septaria, and the rebuilt buttresses and dressings of later stone.

Built between 1270 and 1280 for Sir John de Vallibus, it is essentially a castle keep designed in an 'L' shape, but is also an

Little Wenham Hall.

example of the beginning of the transition from castle to hall in English architecture. The house remains perfectly preserved and is entered in the usual 'defensive' manner at the first floor level. It contains a great hall and vaulted roof chapel dedicated to St Petronilla with a beautiful window and carved figure in the roof. The chapel was possibly completed some time after the main building when Petronilla of Nerford inherited it in 1287.

A footpath skirts the moat and eventually leads to the hall, although there is nothing to see from here. Just glimpses through the trees of newer buildings. On the inside edge of the hall moat is Little Wenham Hall Farm; its fine 16th century brick-nogged timber-framed barn stands next to the church.

LONG MELFORD

—— This is proof-positive that Suffolk is a county of church-shaded villages, built around tranquil greens. Long Melford has one of the biggest at 13 acres, flanked by the stupendous Long

Melford Hall with its pepper-pot turrets where Sir William Cordwell lived stylishly. He founded the not-quite-so-grand Holy Trinity Almshouses in 1573 for twelve poor men, and two good servants. You can find Cordwell's tomb in the church, which should really be called a cathedral, considering it is probably the most magnificent in Suffolk.

In Victorian times, Long Melford was a hive of industry. At the northern end of town, towering above the rooftops of the attractive neighbouring properties, is Coconut House, used in the manufacture of coconut floor matting, and a classic gentleman's residence. At the other end of the social scale, the parish workhouse, one of the largest of its kind in the county, was unfriendly to say the least. Husbands and wives had to contend with only seeing each other in chapel, on Sundays. In his poem *The Village Paupers*, G.W. Fulcher, former Mayor of Sudbury, movingly describes when the 'ruined trader' or 'the hopeless deaf' arrived for Sabbath service. When the workhouse was pulled down in 1839 to make way for the rectory garden, I'm sure a cheer went up!

Author George Borrow is said to have drawn on characters at the workhouse for *Lavengro* (see Oulton). John Tenniel was apparently equally inspired by the superb 15th century stained glass of Elizabeth Talbot in the church, and drew on it for his illustration of the Ugly Duchess, in *Alice in Wonderland*.

The splendid green was the setting, during the 19th century, of the annual Whitsun horse fair; the largest of its kind in East Anglia. It must have been a spectacular sight, as Ernest Ambrose suggests: 'The grand folk and the gentry in their top hats and smart frock coats; the bowler-hatted tradesmen ... the cloth cap workers ... horses, ponies and donkeys poured in by their hundreds, swarming over the lower part of the green' (*Melford Memories*).

The only structure built on the green is a brick conduit, which covered the source of the water supply to Melford Hall in medieval times. It has a spring underneath which regularly springs-forth, sending water flowing along the road. Nearby, on the Westgate Street junction, is the base of the market cross (1555).

LOWESTOFT

The saying goes if you scratch the surface of a local, chances are they are a fisherman, the son of a fisherman or married to one. During the herring fishing boom, in the middle of the last century, there would have been more than 700 trawlers working out of the port, so you could walk across the harbour jumping from deck to deck, if you felt so inclined. The catch today is more likely to be cod or plaice, than the 'silver darlings'.

In 1609 the corporation of Trinity House erected a pair of lights known as the 'High Light' and the 'Low Light' to guide ships through the tricky Stanford channel. From this, Suffolk became the first county systematically to light its coastline. The town was well defended with anti-aircraft batteries and scores of pillboxes when it was a large naval base, and the closest town to Hitler's Germany.

Now tourism is the main industry, thanks in no small way to Sir Samuel Morton Peto who developed the harbour facilities in the town from the 1840s. In five years he built the fish markets and the wharves as well as laying out the open land south of the harbour with a broad esplanade and seaside houses. Directly opposite the entrance to the Harbour is the site of the old Hippodrome, built in 1904 as a music hall, by circus impresario George Gilbert. He was so keen to have the hall up and running that he employed 140 builders to construct the main auditorium in just 14 days, using some 400,000 bricks. The opening acts included such spectacles as the Fat Boy of Peckham, aged 5, who tipped the scales at twelve stones. And we worry about weighty children today.

The old cobbled streets, known as 'scores' (thought to have been formed by footsteps creating paths in the soft sloping cliffs of the beach) with tightly packed houses leading down to the foreshore, were once home to beach families. Three underground cottages, one dating from the 1700s, which came to light this year under the sewing centre in the High Street after lying undisturbed for over half a century, had views of the sea before they were built over. The owner hopes this latest glimpse of old Lowestoft can be turned into a museum.

MARLESFORD

—— A simple memorial in the corner of the church, to Flora Sandes Yudenitch, wife of Colonel Yudenitch and daughter of a former rector Samuel Sandes, made me want to find out more about the first woman ever to hold a commission in the Serbian Army (1916); when she was nearly 40 years old.

When her husband Yuri Yudenitch died, she returned to Suffolk; which must have seemed rather tame after all that action, but at least she had her memories. As one of the entries in her book reads: 'I lay on my back looking up at the stars and when one of them asked me what I was thinking about, I told him that when I was old and decrepit and done for, and had to stay in a house and not go about any more, I should remember my first night with the Fourth Company on the top of Mount Chukus' (*An English Woman-Sergeant in the Serbian Army*). She died in Wickham Market in 1956, aged 80.

The Shuldhams knew a little about war too. Former lord of the manor William Shuldham celebrated his 100th birthday in July 1843, outliving his son, one of the many Scots Grey soldiers killed at the Battle of Waterloo in 1815.

In many respects 'Maerel's Ford' is still feudal in nature. Lord Marlesford, who as one villager euphemistically put it is somewhat 'hands-on', owns most of the properties. The heart of the village is triangular in shape, centred on a cluster of flint and thatched cottages. Opposite the church is the old bowling green and pavilion. Next door is a lovely Georgian rectory where the present rector actually lives.

Follow the road up from the church and a footpath (by a small green) takes you down the side of the 18th century hall with its distinctive green shutters. The ornate gates and gatehouse to the hall, and wonderful spreading cedars in the park, can be seen further along the road, out of the village towards Parham.

MARTLESHAM

—— Fancy a trip to the USA or Scandinavia without leaving the county? You can reach Broomheath down a lane opposite 'California'. The heath is a wildlife sanctuary with splendid views over Martlesham Creek to Kyson Point. You walk among the gorse, with just birds for company and only the faint roar of the traffic to spoil the peace.

By the church, the Norwegian effect takes over, with houses on slopes tumbling down to the creek. This is tree-house country around here. One I saw on the way to the church had collapsed in the recent strong winds. St Mary's has pretty stained glass, some in the Arts & Crafts' style from the beginning of the last century, and memorials to the Doughty family after which the public footpaths, Doughty's Way, are named. At the bottom of the path is the splendid redbrick Martlesham Hall.

St Mary's marks what used to be the village centre; now it is inland near the Red Lion pub. On the front of the old timber-framed coaching inn is a ship's figurehead in the shape of a lion, said to have come from a Dutch boat captured at the Battle of Sole Bay. In 1672, the English fleet of 71 ships and 23,000 men, accompanied by a French fleet, took on the Dutch. Both sides suffered severe casualties, and neither claimed victory.

During the First World War there was an airfield on the heath, and for the next 50 years the site was used as an RAF experimental centre. During the Second World War No 242 Squadron, which included flying ace Sir Douglas Bader, and American airmen from the USAAF 356th Fighter Group, were stationed here. The last planes took off in 1980. It is now the site for BT's research centre; surely one of the ugliest buildings in Suffolk!

MELTON

—— A village proper, or a suburb of Woodbridge? The debate has been going on for years. In some ways the two virtually merge, but Melton led the way in 1897 by getting street lighting before Woodbridge. And court sessions were held at Melton Gaol in the village centre for more than eight centuries, until Thomas Seckford built the Shire Hall in Woodbridge and moved the court there.

In the early 16th century, when the wool trade was declining and civil unrest over mismanagement by the ruling classes was widespread throughout England, a group of rebels set up camp here. The rebels were pacified by the intervention of local noblemen before the potential conflict escalated to the scale seen in Norfolk under Robert Kett.

Three centuries later, Melton was quite a prosperous little town with a foundry, a brewery (bought by Sir Cuthbert Quilter of Bawdsey), a quay and docks at Welford Bridge and a train station and goods yard. St Audrey's Hospital to the north-west of the village was originally designed as a workhouse in 1765 and became the county lunatic asylum in 1827; it closed in 1993.

The late Canon Wilkinson of Melton Grove was possibly less than sane. He is reputed to have kept the mummified head of Oliver Cromwell in his house to show to the curious. The embalmed head came into the Wilkinson family in the 19th century and became a treasured family heirloom. It has been laid to rest at Sidney Sussex College, Cambridge.

Equally dotty behaviour was shown by local builder William Marjoram, who built a tiny castle, Castlecote, in 1895 for his wife. The couple spent their declining years here and following a Zeppelin bombing in 1915, which not surprisingly sent the local population into a complete tizz, he built an air raid shelter in the garden. This brick and flint folly is covered inside with engraved texts and extracts from the Old Testament. You can get a good look at the outside in Bredfield Road. From the traffic lights, head up Bury Hill towards the A12, slow down at Godfrey's Place and it's there on the corner.

 **MENDHAM**

—— The ancient All Saints church stands a few yards from the county boundary with Norfolk. The coats of arms of the two counties can be seen on the bridge spanning the nearby river Waveney. Perhaps the Second World War pill box by the church was left here to ward off Norfolkians who get too close? Waveney does mean 'troubled waters'.

William de Warenne, 1st Earl of Surrey, and his wife Gundreda, William the Conqueror's daughter, established the Cluniac Priory of St Pancras in the marshes but little remains today. Norman arcading from the cell was removed to Mendham Place and the stone recycled for cottages.

New houses abound which makes the mill where Alfred Munnings was born (now private) stand out like a beacon. The best view is from the bridge as you enter the village. Munnings grew up drawing and painting in the idyllic scenery of the surrounding Waveney valley. Cattle grazing in the distant water meadows, willows and poplar trees lining the banks of the interspersing ponds and lakes; the large weatherboarded mill standing guard. Flour has been milled on this site since the earliest records began. Munnings' brother was the last miller.

The young Munnings was surrounded by characters like Richmer, a lame old soldier with piercing eyes and grey side-whiskers, and Fairhead the carpenter whose chisels and planes were an endless fascination for Alfred. So much so that he set up a studio in the old carpenter's shop, painting horses and local characters including a band of gypsies on Mendham Common, which he eventually joined. Charlotte Grey and her pony became *Charlotte's Pony*; the painting is reproduced on the village sign.

I don't think he ever painted Henry Cabell, a thief who was transported to Sydney Cove, Australia. He is evidently the first Englishman to set foot in Sydney Cove, having been elected to carry the ship's captain ashore on his back.

METTINGHAM

—— The ruins and grounds of the castle offer a unique insight to the home of Sir John de Norwich. One of England's first, but little known, great sea commanders, he was Admiral of Edward III's Northern Fleet and Bailiff of Yarmouth.

In 1342 he was rewarded for his services against the Scots, Spaniards and French by being given permission to convert his manor house into a fortified castle. Instead of soldiers, he filled his new home with priests from nearby Raveningham and under the guidance of a priest and thirteen chaplains, young men were prepared for the priesthood. Sir John's coat of arms is on display in the church of All Saints where, as the story goes, he was entombed in the chancel wall after his death in 1363.

The main feature of the castle, which he left to the church, is the gatehouse with its twin towers and arch. In 1842 six silver bells were found in the moat near the site of the old belfry tower. A Dutch family bought the castle a few years ago, and the Dutch tricolour can be seen flying on the village signpost. By way of continuity, Mettingham Hall, built around 1660, a little to the south-east, has beautiful curved Dutch gables and a moat.

MIDDLETON

—— At the turn of the last century, the ritual of the Cutty Wren was played out here every St Stephen's Day, 26th December. After being confined to the local history archives for several decades, it was revived in 1994 as 'Old Glory'. Molly dancing in East Suffolk had new life breathed into it at the same time, for which we are most grateful, of course.

The wren-hunt ritual has its origins in Neolithic times. The Druids were said to have prophesied the future from listening to the song of a captured wren, and some considered it to have powers of darkness as it had a habit of creeping into crevices and caves. On the evening of St Stephen's, the Cutty Wren is solemnly carried from the village hall through the streets by the light of lanterns and flaming torches, arriving at the thatched Bell Inn at nine o'clock. Old Glory then perform dances in honour of the Wren. Molly dancing is thought to be the East Anglian form of Morris dancing, characterised by black faces, and heavy hobnailed boots, the normal footwear for farmworkers at the early part of 20th century.

Dancing was probably not encouraged on the seven acre moor, a mile from the Bell along the Causeway and said to be the only moor in Suffolk, but such gyrations might have improved the circulation of the poor souls baptised by immersion in the pond (since dried up) in 1908. The moor is now owned by the county council, although some householders skirting the edge of the grassy field have long-standing privileges, such as the right to gather hay.

The lead-covered needle spire of Holy Trinity draws you back to the village centre. Inside the Arms of George III ('mad King George'), unusually cast in iron, stands next to a fine Perpendicular window. The five ancient bells strike every hour and were recast in London in 1779, returning to Middleton by sea, via Aldeburgh. The Minsmere river passes through the village outskirts en route to the marshes and bird sanctuary. A small smock drainage mill that stood on the Minsmere Level finally gave up the ghost in 1977. It was rescued by volunteers, rebuilt and is now at the Museum of East Anglian Life, Stowmarket.

MILDEN

—— It might seem strange that a village should take its name from what today is considered to be a weed, but in Anglo-Saxon times, Milden was known by the name of the plant which grew profusely in the area – 'Melde'. This edible species, *Chenopodum*

Album commonly known as 'Fat Hew', can still be found in fields and gardens and is said to be rich in calcium, iron and vitamin B1. As described at the entrance to the church, this most valuable vegetable for humans and animals alike was too desirable a crop to be ignored by food-seeking tribes.

A tribe came here during the 5th to 7th centuries, liked what they saw, feasted on the weed and decided to stay, designating the area 'Meldinga'. The name has changed quite a few times down the centuries, with 17 different versions until finally, in the 17th century, something approximating to the name today, 'Mildin'.

The Norman church on a windswept hillside has lovely views over the valley of the Lavenham brook and stands near the eastern boundary of this large parish. St Peter's church has an excellent Jacobean pulpit and a fine recumbent alabaster effigy of a former lord of the manor, James Allington. In the 17th century, the Rev William Burkitt lived here and his *Expository Notes on the New Testament* was at one time recognised as an outstanding work of its kind.

At the Drury Lane junction with Church Road, look through the hedge to your right to spot the remains of a moat. It is part of the 18th century Milden Hall with Venetian windows in the centre. Near the hall is a motte with what might be the remains of its bailey. Perhaps it was one of the defences thrown up unofficially while arguments over who should succeed to the throne were being fought out between Matilda and King Stephen, during his turbulent reign in the mid 1100s.

MONK SOHAM

—— Robert Hindes Groome (there is a picture of him at the back of the church) succeeded his father as rector in 1845 and was a busy little bee over the next 44 years, building the rectory-house and the school, as well as restoring the church. The yews by the churchyard gates were a present to him from Edward Fitzgerald, the other subject of *Two Suffolk Friends*, a nostalgic look at Victorian central Suffolk, written by Groome's son Francis.

Monk Soham had 400 inhabitants then. Before the Reformation it was a daughter house of St Edmund's Abbey and the place where refractory monks were sent for some country air. (Hence its name, the 'south village of the monks'.) Maybe they enjoyed watching pike and roach splashing among the reeds and water-lilies in the rectory fish ponds, as Groome did. He would blandish them: 'Fish, fish do your duty'.

Not only could he talk to our aquatic friends, but Groome was a past-master in Suffolk people-speak. Only once was he stumped by a Suffolk phrase. The occasion was when a small boy in class had been put in the corner. 'What for?' asked Groome, and a chorus of voices answered: 'He has 'bin tittymatauterin'. Which means, apparently, he had been playing see-saw. But then we all knew that, didn't we?

The large east window of St Peter's is supposed to have come from Bury Abbey and gives a rather fine view of the surrounding farmlands and the oaks, elms, beeches and limes, planted by Robert in the grounds of the old rectory, half a mile away. You can spot the odd Tudor rose emblem in the church as well as at Monk Soham Hall, next door. It is a sad irony that it would take a Tudor king to dissolve this monastery, as well as countless others across the land.

MONKS ELEIGH

—— As lovely as nearby Lavenham without the madding crowds. It's even got a guildhall and a Swan hostelry to rival Lavenham's. There has been a settlement in Monks Eleigh since the Stone Age (c.3500 BC) and artefacts from this period have been found at Slough Farm. Documents dating back to Aelfgar, who was lord of the manor until his death in AD 953, were also unearthed.

Despite its name the village has never been a home to monks, although the manor was bequeathed to the monks of Canterbury by Aelfgar's son-in-law Beorhtnoth, and belonged to them until the last century. The title is now in the hands of the church of St Peter where a 'rogues gallery' of former rectors makes a nice change from one long list of names.

The hall, dating from 1658, is fairly modest with the initials MB on the chimneystack, referring to Puritan Miles Burkitt who bought the hall when the Dean and Chapter were temporarily expropriated during the Commonwealth. He rebuilt the hall only to find himself in the same position when Charles II took the throne. Hobarts was home to the Hobart family, including Sir James who was to become Attorney General to Henry VII.

Elizabeth walking home to Monks Eleigh in the mist.

The Brett runs through Monks Eleigh splitting the village in two: The Street, and Swingleton Green with its thatched and timbered houses. Elizabeth, daughter of the owner of the manor farm, became lost in the mist while walking along the banks of the river Brett. The story goes that with night drawing in, and fearing she would not make it home, she fortuitously heard the welcoming chimes of the church clock. She followed the sound, and on each quarter was able to correct her bearings until, eventually, she found her way home. On hearing the story her father pledged to give a meadow to the church to pay for the upkeep of the clock (Clock Meadow). How sweet.

Corner Farmhouse at Brent Eleigh, 16th century (with some Victorianisation) and Grade II listed, stands, naturally, on a corner among leafy lanes. It has no less than 30 handmade wooden doors, all different, and one of them is only three feet high. Not somewhere to try to enter in the mist.

MOULTON

—— It would certainly be easy to feel rootless here; no more graphically illustrated than in Station Road where one minute you're in Suffolk, the next in Cambridgeshire. The roads are narrowed for the benefit of horse and rider from the studlands of nearby Kentford.

Packhorses used to cross the picturesque 15th century hump-backed bridges over the river Kennet; in particular the more northerly of the two with its impressive four arches. Built of flint with each arch lined in brick, it used to carry traffic from Cambridge to Bury. According to the English Heritage information alongside, medieval packhorse bridges were found in areas where the roads were not sufficiently good for wheeled vehicles. Goods and people could only be transported on the backs of animals; hence the narrow packhorse bridge. Despite its name, Moulton Bridge, strictly speaking, probably wasn't used by packhorses, since it is just wide enough to take a cart.

In fact, there are various crossings, such as the Old Flint Bridge, also 15th century, close to Brookside. There is also a wooden bridge, and an iron one. You could easily spend the whole day criss-crossing this village of wide meadows, flints and thatches.

A quick hop over the A14 takes you into Tuddenham, a Breckland village lying among what is considered to be some of the most vertically challenged land in Suffolk. In the past it was said that a man could plough in a straight line for 20 furlongs. Maybe this is good for flowers, as the area boasts some unique wild species, including the wonderfully named 'Fingered Speedwell' and 'Rupture Wort'.

NAYLAND & WISSINGTON

—— Both villages lie beside the Stour at the beginning of its prettiest upper reach and have a habit of being spoken of in one and the same breath. Nayland, a market and cloth-making centre with a good crop of timber-framed houses; Wissington a green farming parish.

In the 16th century, Nayland produced light, serge-like cloths to try to stay competitive but the fight was lost to the dark satanic mills in the north of England. Fen Street, to the north of the market square off Church Street, has a charming group of houses set back behind a stream, each with its own bridge and probably once occupied by cloth workers. Abels Bridge dates from 1959, but a 16th century brick version was built by wealthy clothier John Abel for the navigation of barges. You can just make out a small 'A' and a bell on the keystone.

Everything in Wissington, or 'Wiston', is on a small scale.

Wiston Hall was built in 1791 for a former director of the Bank of England, Samuel Beechcroft. St Mary's church is more or less in its garden. Paintings, said to be 13th century, adorn the walls in the nave, one of which is thought to be the earliest representation, in English art, of St Francis. Over the door is a dragon dating from when such mythical creatures were all the rage in the Stour valley. There is a handsome weatherboarded watermill on the river to match the weatherboarded bell-turret of the church.

The memorial in St Mary's to the four men killed on the fields of northern France, in the First World War, is especially poignant. On a nearby hill is the East Anglian Sanatorium started by Dr Jane Walker, who pioneered 'fresh air' treatment for tuberculosis, while living in France. The air felt fresh enough when I visited the parish, with just peewits flying high in black and white flocks, to keep me company.

NEEDHAM MARKET

—— The river Gipping was navigable, here, as far back as the 12th century when it was used to bring the Caen stone for the fabrication of Bury St Edmunds Abbey. The Ipswich and Stowmarket Navigation Act of 1790 led to the building of 15 locks, which raised the barges some 27 metres over the 17 miles of the navigation. You can find more of this Norman stone in the Suffolk red-bricked railway station; built between 1846 and 1849, closed in the 1960s, and reopened later under public pressure.

The Limes Hotel, a fine timber-framed building with an 18th century red-brick Georgian facade, was used by pilgrims in the Middle Ages as a calling house on their way to Bury. The 18th century also saw the building of the Quaker meeting house. Needham Market was an important centre for the Society of Friends for several generations. Members of the Alexanders, a pioneering Quaker family, are buried in the grounds.

Frederick Barnes designed the old town hall, built in 1866, in the Italianate style. The first floor had a large room for public concerts, lectures and meetings, and the ground floor was a police station with cells and a court room to the rear; in case anyone over-stepped the mark, perhaps? Over the entrance is a stone tablet engraved with the date and the names of the patron, architect and builder.

The chain bridge to the west, and Chain House Farm to the east, are reminders of when the plague was rife. Chains were erected across the road at these points beyond which nobody could cross. Food was exchanged for money, the coins of which were sterilised in vinegar. The poor souls afflicted were buried in a mass grave outside the village on a site that is now a housing estate; news which I bet would thrill the residents no end!

NEWBOURNE

—— Others might have done, and still do, but Nebrunaa didn't. Give this village a miss, that is. The Dane stayed and gave his name, meaning new spring; the nearby nature reserve is renowned for several springs.

The Land Settlement Act changed the character of Nebrunaa's village dramatically in the 1930s. Near the village hall is a group of cottages with greenhouses and allotments. These were set up by the government and the Carnegie Trust to provide new hope for unemployed miners from Yorkshire and Durham; some of whom had been on the historic Jarrow Crusade ('hunger march for jobs') of 1936. Each was given a small yellow-brick house, two windows long, along with two greenhouses and five acres of land to grow vegetables or flowers. Some couldn't cope with the rural way of life and left. Others became members of the Land Association, which was wound up in 1983.

Living off a healthy diet from the land probably helped produce giants among men. In the churchyard is the grave and headstone (third on the left as you come out of church) of George Page who was said to be 7ft 6in tall. He and his brother Meadows, only a couple of inches shorter, were known as 'The Newbourne Giants'. They were spotted at the 1868 Easter Fair in Woodbridge and given contracts to tour the regions as the fair's latest curiosity.

Their house, appropriately called 'Giants House', is next door to the pub where Chieftain, a stallion, apparently regularly 'drank' a quart of beer. The pub's beer garden can also boast the last remaining traditional skittle alley in the whole of the county – a 20 foot long lane made of boards.

During the 1987 hurricane, the church's east wall was blown out leaving the stained glass window in pieces. A new window was dedicated a couple of years later and included the only recognisable piece of the original glass, the face of Christ.

NEWMARKET

In the 14th century there were prohibitions against holding tournaments. Three centuries later James I was to change this through his interest in blood sports, particularly coursing, hunting and hawking the great bustard; a bird last seen in this area in 1840. James organised the first horse race in 1619, and so began the 'sport of kings', taken to new heights by Charles II.

Another James got lucky. Lenwade Hall on the Bury road was built at the beginning of the last century, as the dream home of James Larnoch. He was able to afford his pile after his horse 'Djeddah' won the Derby in 1898 at odds of 100-1. It is now a horse and animal hospital run by the Animal Health Trust, the only charitable organisation devoted to the diagnosis, cure and prevention of animal disease. They welcome visitors, and willing helpers!

The Start at Newmarket; Study No. 4 earned the artist Munnings 1.1 million dollars at a Sotheby's auction in New York. His great love was horses and the racing scene, and he was a regular visitor to Newmarket. He used a rubbing-down house on the edge of the July Course as a studio, where he enhanced his reputation with studies of the Newmarket start line.

Joseph the Gypsy Boy's reputation was shattered when a sheep in his care went missing. The story goes that the penalty for such a crime in 19th century England was death; he hanged himself. As he had taken his own life, he couldn't be given a Christian burial in the churchyard, so was buried on the side of the road instead. A simple cross beside the Bury road marks the spot. Each year flowers are left anonymously, the colours said to predict those worn by the winning jockey on Derby Day.

The great course on the heath lies west of the town, on the Cambridgeshire border, flanked by the most spectacular earthwork defence, the Devil's Dyke, which once ran from the marshy area of Reach to the wooded area of Stetchworth.

NEWTON

At one time there were four Newtons in Suffolk, so the appendage 'Green' was attached in the 1930s to help His Majesty's Postal Office sort out all the mail. Richard Neville, Earl of Warwick, known as 'the Kingmaker', and at one time

Lord of the Manor here might have received his fair share of hate mail. During the turbulent years of Henry VI's rule (1422-61) he effectively governed England, and was a staunch defender of his saintly, but ineffectual, master. King and mentor were later to quarrel and Neville switched his allegiance to the House of Lancaster in a desperate bid to preserve his personal power. He died a bloody death at the Battle of Barnet in 1471.

Life today is more serene, and current battles are likely to centre on mastering the consistently frustrating game of golf, rather than civil strife. The village sign depicts an oak divided diagonally by a golf club, referring to the links course which covers the green; quite a distracting sight as you drive down the main street, watching the drivers and putters cursing the day they ever took up their clubs. Equally challenging to your concentration are some of the breath-taking houses that line Links Road. One particularly fine timber-framed building has a Jacobean glass front window depicting three men in what resembles medieval garb.

Also shown on the sign are two sacks of coal; one of the founder members of the Golf Club was a coal merchant who gave each resident 2 cwts of coal in exchange for use of the common for his sport. The fee was later changed to 2 lb of tea; but no sugar.

Life as the local parson must have been sweet though; the church retained the same rector, Charles Smith, for 61 years. The pretty 14th century flint and timber All Saints church has a lovely covered porch and impressive wooden doors. Definitely more in keeping with East Anglia, than, I suspect, Utah. The Dansie family of Salt Lake City in memory of their daughter Charlotte, who married here in 1849, donated a board at the entrance to the church. There is also a headstone in the churchyard to a man who 'smiled through life'. Maybe one fine day he managed to sink a hole in one?

NORTON

A thousand years ago, Norton was known as 'Nocturne'; the 'King's land' after Godric. In the early 16th century it became famous for a brief period when another monarch, Henry VIII, decided to pan for gold here, but to no avail. Prospect Road, a modern estate opposite the heath is the only hint of when times looked good for the village, albeit temporarily.

Norton was always spread out, with villagers having grazing rights to the heathlands, but records show that as early as the 15th century, Littlehaugh Manor had nearly 200 cases of enclosure. With the Enclosure Act of 1814, the villagers' grazing rights to the remaining heathland were removed altogether and, by way of compensation, allotments were allocated where some of the houses in Heath Road now stand.

Half a mile down the Ixworth road is Little Haugh Hall dating from 1730, although the entrance is 19th century. It was built for Cox Macro (1683-1757), an antiquarian son of a rich grocer from Bury, who became a student of medicine and chaplain to George II. The park and lakes enclose a tributary stream of the Little Ouse. About a mile from the central crossroads in the village is another house fit for a king; the stunning Grade II listed timber-framed and thatched High Hall.

ORFORD

—————— This coastal strip of shingle bank is, strictly speaking, only temporary as it has only been formed over the past few hundred years, is constantly changing and is liable to disappear again in a storm or if erosion continues at its steady rate. Maps from the mid-1800s show the shingle bank, which now reaches Shingle Street, stopping opposite Orford village; with Havergate Island out in the sea forming the south side of a harbour entrance.

Orford Ness is one of the most remarkable natural features along the coast, measuring nine miles and home to sea birds like avocets, shelducks, oyster catchers, sandwich terns, redshanks, plovers and geese. It was an important military area during both world wars and remained a top-secret testing station through to the 1980s. The 'pagodas' left behind were designed for rapid collapse in the event of a nuclear attack.

Henry II built the castle in 1165 to stop his barons attempting an attack on his authority. The castle changed hands frequently during the 13th century Barons' Wars but by 1336 it was granted, in perpetuity, to Robert of Ufford, Earl of Suffolk. The dungeons aren't utilised these days, but in 1270 they were host to the legendary wild man of the sea who had been caught in fishing nets. Stuart Bacon, of the Suffolk Underwater Studies Group, based in the village, has described him as a 'mer-man', and someone of stern stuff to endure so much time in the unforgiving North Sea.

Attempting to catch smugglers 'owling' along this stretch of coast was something of a sport for customs and excise officers in the 17th century. Smuggling wool to the continent was rife, and not without mishap, as described in Richard Cobbold's novel (see Brandeston). A trap was laid by positioning 14 officers, fortified by rum, at 500 yard intervals along the beach with only their heads appearing above the shingle. The password was 'King George for ever' with the response 'Hurrah!' A ship was seen anchoring, the boat rowed onto the shingle and the officers moved in. A fair cop, surely.

OTLEY

In 1602 Bartholomew Gosnold of Otley Hall led an exploratory expedition of 32 men aboard the ship *Concord* to the coast of 'the north parts of Virginia' in America. He landed at Cape Cod, explored the area and named Martha's Vineyard after his wife and daughter who shared the same name. In 1607, some 13 years before the Pilgrim Fathers' historic sailing, he set off again with a larger party to create the first permanent settlement from England in the New World. The place they finally chose became Jamestown, Virginia.

A ghost is said to haunt the grounds of the partly-moated, timber and brick hall. In 1930 a cook mysteriously drowned in the moat where black swans used to float by. Duckings, rather than drownings used to take place in the 13th century St Mary's church which has a rare immersion font, one of only two in the country, below the floor of the vestry.

It is approximately 7 feet long by 4 feet wide and 2 feet 8 inches deep and is said to have been used in the mid 17th century by Anabaptists, a Protestant sect of early 16th century German origin, who believed that baptism should be confined to adults only. When I paid a visit to the church, the captain of the bellringers told me that during a charity event a local offered to retrieve any 'lucky' coins thrown in. He dived in naked and lived to tell the tale. Fortunately the water is not stagnant and is topped up regularly with water from the church roof. The font was probably a means of keeping Anabaptists within the one Church of Christ. The local Strict Baptist chapel was built in 1800, so the use of the font must predate that.

Rich farmland drains south into Otley Bottom where

earthworks of a Norman castle stand beside the line of the Roman road. You can see the barrow from the back of the church if you look across the fields to a clump of trees. There is an even better view from the top of the church tower where you might also be able to spot the attractive, timber-framed High House half a mile to the east, built around the same time as the hall, c.1500.

OULTON & OULTON BROAD

—— The distinctive octagonal sign shows author George Borrow's cottage and a brass rubbing of Sir John Fastolfe, which can also be seen in the Norman church of St Michael, where he is buried. Sir John built Caister Castle in Norfolk, between 1432 and 1435, one of the last licensed castles erected in England. He also became unjustly branded a figure of fun when Shakespeare first took his name for the character of Sir John Falstaff in Henry IV: 'Falstaff sweats to death and lards the lean earth as he walks along'. He was, in fact, very much a hero gaining numerous battle honours, and leading the archers at the Battle of Agincourt in 1415.

Such character assassination never beset Norfolk-born author George Borrow, famous for his romantic accounts of everyday gypsy life. He wrote a number of his books in his octagonal summerhouse (now gone) in the garden on the north-west shore of the Broad. He was always a traveller and would regularly set off on 'walks' that would take him all over the British Isles, not appearing home for months. On one occasion, he walked from Norwich to London, 112 miles, in 27 hours. Closer to home, he would cut a dash in his Spanish cloak and broad-brimmed hat on walks around the Broads. His connections with the area live on in a pub in Oulton Broad named after him, which would have raised a smile:

'Good ale, the true and proper drink of Englishmen.
He is not deserving of the name of Englishman who
speaketh against ale, that is good ale.'
                    – George Borrow, *Lavengro* ch. 48

Feel like some jibing and tacking? The International Sailing Craft Association (ISCA) has 160 rare and ethnic boats making up the largest collection in the world, including Italian gondola and Arab dhow. These wooden craft need sailing to keep them ship-shape, and the museum is happy for competent crew to take them out for an afternoon's sail.

✿ PAKEFIELD

—— Crime writer P. D. James, or rather Baroness James of Holland Park of Southwold in the County of Suffolk to give her proper title, often spent her summer holidays camping here when she lived in Cambridge. Maybe she saw murder and mystery in those brooding East Anglian skies, and sometimes wild seas.

As the author once told me: 'I don't think Suffolk is necessarily a sinister place, although some parts of it, like the ruined abbeys, can be very sinister at night. But it's the loneliness of much of Suffolk that inspires me. Just hearing the gulls and the sounds of the waves on the shingle. It has that emptiness and sense of history which I think is tremendously important for a writer.'

The power of the sea has wreaked havoc on this suburb of Lowestoft, with almost half of the original village now swallowed up. In the late 19th century, the Jolly Sailors was set back in the village; now it stands on the cliff edge. There used to be two churches side by side and until 1748, two rectors. The wall dividing the churches was opened up with a series of arches, one of which survived German attack.

In 1941, two incendiary bombs landed on the thatched roof of St Margaret and All Saints. The rector and parishioners managed to dislodge only one and the church burned down. Which probably has something to do with the old song: 'The roaring boys of Pakefield, oh how they all do thrive; they had but one poor parson and him they buried alive!'

The POWs got off comparatively lightly. They were imprisoned in the grounds of Pakefield Hall in a holiday camp built in the 1930s by Howard Barrett, an entrepreneur from London, and now Pontins.

The ghost of local girl 'Crazy Mary' is said to haunt a deep hollow just beyond the remains of the old lighthouse. Mary fell in love with a visiting sailor and on the day before he was due to set sail, they walked along the beach to the spot. She swore to go there every day to look for his ship, but she eventually lost hope. Her body was found washed up on the shore.

—— One of the upper windows of the old vicarage, now called Mulberry House after the tree in the grounds, has a trompe l'oeil by Rex Whistler who was stationed nearby during the Second World War, created just before his death in Normandy. The 'Whistler Window' has been framed and glazed and is of an 18th century parson, in his wig, reading by candlelight. Whistler was a quick worker; apparently he painted it in under an hour.

Sir Walter Greene took rather longer to rebuild Nether Hall, the village's number one house, in 1874. It is said that the earth bank between the hall and The Lodge, known as 'Spiteful Bank', was built by Sir Walter after a quarrel with Sir Compton Thornhill of The Lodge, so that he did not have to see him from his home. The fine Jacobean Newe House, from 1622, a completely symmetrical building with a brick facade, three Dutch gables and mullioned windows, is a sight for any eyes.

On a ridge of the Blackbourne valley, at Grimstone End, two miles north, is the parish watermill and windmill, lying within half a mile of each other. The claim is still made that they are the only working ones, lying so close together, in Britain. 'Ticking over', would be a more accurate description. The watermill carries a datestone, 1814, but the foundations of a Tudor mill are preserved underground. The windmill was erected in around 1830 and was used regularly until the 1950s. It used to be nearer the old turnpike road, but was deemed to be too close, and moved a quarter of a mile further along the Ixworth road. When there was little wind, one of the Bryant family, who have owned the mills since 1885, would plead with 'Betsy', as she was affectionately known, to turn her sails. They don't need to bother now that it is electrically driven. Its rare copper cap should be back in place anytime now.

Puttocks Hill near the boundary with Great Livermere is where Charles I was said to fly his falcons. Puttock is an old word for a falcon, and the king's falconer is buried in Great Livermere churchyard.

Suffolk might not have any real hills, but it sure does have some deep valleys. Don't take my word for it though. Leave your car at the flint and stone church and head up the sloping churchyard to the brow of the hill and savour the view reminiscent of a Thomas Hardy novel. Watermeadows, grazing sheep, and a cute church nestling in the valley. It's hard to imagine the old USAAF airfield, now an award-winning museum to the 390th Bomb Group, is just down the road. Press on further over a couple of stiles, with considerate 'dog gates' and you hit on Parham's hidden gem: the spectacular timber-framed Moat Hall.

Built as a home for Sir Christopher Willoughby in the early 16th century, its substantial moat and four-centred arched gateway, with a niche either side carved with woodwose, or mythical 'wild men', could easily have been the inspiration for the line, 'an Englishman's home is his castle'. At one time, one of the entrances to the hall had a beautiful stone arch with carved shields, but this caught the eye of an American who bought it in 1926 and shipped it across the Atlantic, London-Bridge style, for the folks back home to admire.

Moat Hall.

I am not sure what they would have made of the original village stocks, mounted inside the thatched lychgate roof of the 14th century church. There are other throwbacks to this volatile period in England's history. As the church guide tells us, in 1383, Walter Manton of Wrotham, William Screvenor of Marlesford and Roger Powel of Eyke, rounded-up some 100 'disaffected souls' and staged their own Peasants' Revolt, rampaging through the village and looting the house of the then rector John Markaant, demanding a fine to save his church from destruction. He paid up, and his name is in the list of incumbents displayed inside the church, not far from the organ pillars with splendid graffiti, reliably dated to 1400, of men in a ship which apparently sailed up the river Ore to Parham.

PEASENHALL

Driving along the main street, now a conservation area, without getting too distracted from the road ahead and careering into the stream which runs the length of the street, is tricky. It is probably best to leave your car in one of the convenient stopping points along the way, for closer inspection of some of the fine buildings. Among the finest must be the timber-framed wool hall known as the New Inn, painstakingly restored and now in the hands of the Landmark Trust and open for view. The Trust also owns the next door tea rooms, with walls adorned (if that is the right word) with framed newspaper cuttings about the infamous murder.

If you're wondering why there is a Swiss chalet here, the explanation is fairly straightforward. One of Peasenhall's most famous sons was James Smyth, renowned for his design and manufacture of the internationally-successful agricultural seed drill. His grandson James Josiah, after a visit to Switzerland, was so taken with the country that he built the Swiss-style chalet hall in the village, as a reading room for company employees. Work stopped at James Smyth & Sons in 1967, but not before the drills, emblazoned with the words 'James Smyth – London, Paris, Peasenhall', had found their way to all parts of the globe.

Now back to the murder of which much has been written but no murderer found. It is back in June 1902. Rose Harsent, a maid at Providence House (now Stuart House) and with child, is brutally murdered. The finger points to William Gardiner, a married man and father of six children, and a fellow member of the Primitive Methodist connection. He is arrested at his house less than 200 yards along the street. An inquest is held at the Swan pub; an adjourned hearing takes place at the Assembly Rooms, at the Hackney Road and Bruisyard junction, and then the first trial at Ipswich with one H.F. Dickens, son of the famous author, as counsel to the prosecution. The police bungle their investigation, witnesses are shown to be unreliable and the jury acquits Gardiner. At the anniversary of her death, the skies are said to darken. Rose is apparently buried in the churchyard close to the path to the church door, which is lined with trees bent double, although I failed to find the grave.

PLAYFORD

The Fynn once flowed into the 10 foot wide moat at Playford Hall. The house is less grand now but sections of the original Elizabethan red-brick mansion remain, and the gardens are rather splendid. A former resident and eminent Knight, Sir George Felbrigge, lives on in brass form in the mainly 14th century church standing high above the north banks of the steep-sided valley. The church is generally locked so don't bother walking up the steep steps to the top to find out. Collect the key first; details on the notice board. Disabled access is best further up the hill where you can park to the rear.

An obelisk in the churchyard in memory of Thomas Clarkson is inscribed 'the friend of slaves'. He was a founder member of the Society for the Abolition of the Slave Trade.

Another inspiring figure, Sir George Biddell Airy (1801-92), Astronomer Royal, lived at Airy's Cottage opposite the lovely lychgate; maybe he climbed to the top of the church tower for a closer look at the stars? Sir George was director of the Greenwich Royal Observatory for 46 years and his work included extensive research on eclipses and magnetism. He was also involved with the international agreement of 1884 establishing the Greenwich Meridian; the international basis of time-reckoning.

Some of the cottages were built by Arthur Biddell, High Constable and land agent, for estate workers, using bricks from Woodbridge Barracks when it was sold in around 1815. He was a tenant of the (then) 400-year-old Hill House, across the fields from Playford Hall.

POLSTEAD

The Romans brought the cherries here. Thriller writer Ruth Rendell, who used to live in a fine old house on the edge of the village, reckons the best time to see the Polstead Black in bloom is the last week of April, when a fluffy white veil covers the village like powder snow. Why the affinity with cherries? One theory is that Polstead is sheltered at the junction of steep wooded tributaries to the Box. In the 1940s, as many as ten lorries would be lined up to collect cherries for sale in surrounding towns. Now you might find the occasional tree in a garden.

In 1827 Polstead was the setting for a home-grown thriller story, 'The Murder in the Red Barn'. The story goes that Maria Marten, who lived in a small thatched cottage south-east of Bell's Corner, ran off with William Corder who lived at Street Farm at the foot of the hill. Six months later, Maria's step-mother dreamed that Maria hadn't eloped but was buried under the floor of the Red Barn, so called because it turned that colour in the setting sun; it burned down in 1842.

She was right and Corder, the prime suspect, was traced to London, arrested and brought back to spend his last night in an upper room at Cock Farm which faces Polstead Green. He was publicly hanged at Bury St Edmunds for her murder, in August 1828. The records of his trial were bound in a book (at Moyse's Hall, Bury) made of his skin and the hangman's rope was sold for a guinea an inch. Maria is buried in the churchyard, her headstone almost chipped away by souvenir hunters.

The Old Rectory is one of five in Suffolk to be faced with 'mathematical tiles', the kind that are imitation white bricks, pallid and anaemic, which could be nailed to a timber frame. The church has the only stone spire in Suffolk and possibly the earliest example of English brick in the chancel and nave. Georgian Polstead Hall has pale-coloured bricks. Between it and the church are the remains of a large oak tree, known as the Gospel Oak after Bishop Cedd who preached beneath it in the 7th century. It had a girth of some 36 feet and was around 1,200 years old.

RATTLESDEN

—— It takes a willing suspension of disbelief to imagine this village, standing on one of the sources of the river Gipping, once earned the epithet, 'The Port of Bury St Edmunds'. The Gipping travels to Stowmarket and Ipswich and then, as the Orwell, reaches the sea at Felixstowe. As late as the 13th century, barges of considerable size made their way up the winding river from the Orwell. Caen stone was brought here by river to build the Abbey Church at Bury. Now the tributary is no more than a brook.

Founded by the monks of Bury, St Nicholas' has a wonderful setting and from its sloping churchyard has a view over plastered houses and cottages, several of which have thatched roofs. A black and white half-timbered house (old Moot Hall) stands beside the lower churchyard gate. It is worth making a trip to the other side of the valley to view this church in its setting, a scene that I defy you not to drool over.

A plaque in the north aisle of the church keeps alive the memory of Richard Kimball (1595-1675) whose family lived at Hitcham and who married Ursula Scott of Rattlesden. The couple sailed in 1634 aboard the Ipswich vessel *Elizabeth* to New England.

The sign is surrounded by two whale bones, which can be seen next to the bridge. Such bones were often erected as ornaments in the 19th century in a number of villages. Perhaps they just had a surplus of corsets. Timber-framed Clopton Hall, on the shoulder of the hill, which has a date of 1681 on one of the chimneys, stands on an early settlement site with natural springs. The north front was built by Colonel John Fiske, who had been at the Siege of Colchester in 1648 (where captives had to eat cats and dogs to survive), and the south front by Colonel Windsor Parker, who was beleaguered at the Siege of Bhurtpore in 1825.

REDGRAVE & HOPTON

—— Arachnophobes are not encouraged. The Redgrave and Lopham Fen is the only area in the British Isles that is home to the rare Great Raft Spider (*dolomedes fimbiatus*) which is capable of catching small fish below the water surface.

Aside from this claim to fame, Redgrave is quite unusual in being the source of two rivers, the Waveney and the Little Ouse, which run in opposite directions. The now demolished Redgrave

Hall dominates its history. In 1211 the manor was in the hands of Abbot Samson of Bury for whom the first hall was built. At the Dissolution it passed to the Bacon family. Sir Nicholas Bacon, father of philosopher and scientist Francis Bacon, was solicitor of the Court of Augmentations, which disposed of monastic properties, and later Lord Keeper of the Seal to Elizabeth I.

In the late 17th century, the hall was sold to Sir John Holt, Lord Chief Justice of the King's Bench, who had it rebuilt. It was demolished in 1960, though the grey brick octagonal gatehouse with a 1767 dome survives, which you can see from the road, along with the lake and some fine oaks. There is a memorial at the entrance to the park to the 65th General Hospital US Army who were stationed here in 1944/5, and where thousands were treated after the D-Day landings.

There are fine monuments to both Bacon (1616) and Holt (1709) in the 14th century church of St Mary the Virgin. Rowland Holt was responsible for rebuilding much of the church when Thomas Wolsey was supposedly rector in 1506. The Hart family, local organ builders, claimed Mendelssohn among their customers; perhaps they built the one for the church?

At nearby Hopton, the new Angles Way passes through the eastern edge of the fen where reeds for thatching are still cut. The nave clerestory of the 14th century All Saints is of Tudor brick with a striking late medieval hammerbeam roof. The five daughters of a Victorian vicar apparently painted it.

REDLINGFIELD

—— It is hard to imagine sombre figures from the past could be associated with this charming village with some fine farmhouses, including Redlingfield Hall Farm, which adjoins the church of St Andrew, and was built on the site of a former nunnery.

The flint barn and fragments of windows are all that remain of the Benedictine nunnery founded in 1120 by the Count of Guisnes and his wife Emma who was the daughter of William de Arras, Lord of Redlingfield. The order was dedicated to the 'Honour of God and the Blessed Apostle of St Andrew', and it was not without its scandals. According to records from 1427, the Prioress admitted that she had not attended mass or confession for a couple of years, and that she had been alone with Thomas Langelong, a bailiff, 'in private and suspicious circumstances'. She resigned, but the whole convent still had to fast on bread and beer on Fridays; perhaps not much of a penance if you are into your ale. With the Dissolution, all the lands belonging to the nunnery were turned over to Sir Edmund Bedingfield, and the inmates were turned out; a sad moment depicted on the village sign.

The water for making the penitents' beer no doubt came from one of the many ponds. Despite heavy losses since the Second World War, Suffolk has more than 22,000 rural ponds and recent research by English Nature showed that Redlingfield is one of the 'pond centres' of the county, with ten times the British average for the number of ponds per square kilometre of land. All within Suffolk's heavy clay belt, the ponds were once numerous; the result of the 19th century farming system where livestock were kept in relatively small fields. Every village green and farmyard also needed a pond to water the work horses. A pond warden scheme is being considered to make sure ponds don't disappear, and that endangered creatures such as great crested newts are safeguarded.

RENDLESHAM

—— In 1687 a silver crown, reputed to have been Raedwald's, weighing 60oz was dug up at a place called Thirstly Belt near a cluster of trees and a shallow ditch on the way to Campsea Ashe. Was this the site of the Wuffingas' court? It would be nice to think so. Raedwald is said to have ruled from AD 599 to 625 and was responsible, after a visit to King Ethelbert of Kent in 617, for the introduction of Christianity to East Anglia.

There isn't much point searching out Rendlesham Hall, built in 1871, with grounds laid out by Humphry Repton; it was demolished in 1949. But three of its five lodges survive, two of which were built as follies in 1790; Ivy Lodge, a mock-Norman ruin with big archways and a low turret (see Tunstall) and Woodbridge Lodge with its distinctly Gothic feel and three flying buttresses supporting a chimney, with a cottage attached. You can just about see it from the Snape-Woodbridge road on the edge of Bentwaters airfield.

The Grade I listed Wantisden church, only metres away from the perimeter fence of Bentwaters, has a tower built entirely of coralline crag limestone, one of only two examples, along with Chillesford, of its kind in England. The crag is usually tobacco-coloured and is made up of sea mats (*bryozoa*) and fossilised sea shells (*mollusca*) embedded in sands and low cliffs between Butley and Aldeburgh millions of years ago.

When alien forces once roamed the land perhaps? On Christmas Night 1980, the civil aviation base at Watton tracked an unidentified object on its radar, picking up the reading over the Wash and losing it over Rendlesham Forest. At RAF Woodbridge, a front line NATO base, three security guards spotted strange lights in the forest. They later described seeing a triangular object, around nine feet high with a series of lights around it. It moved away leaving depressions on the ground where it had landed. An orange glow was spotted two days later in the trees. Evidently the crew of HMS *Norfolk*, anchored off Orford Ness, was ordered to stay below decks and keep all the power turned off. Jenny Randles has written a book on the subject: *UFO Crash Landing? Friend or Foe.* To see for yourself, organised walks are arranged in July. Watch the press for details. Or should that read, the sky?

REYDON

—— At one time 'buss' boats – small, two-masted fishing vessels, built using oaks from the nearby wood – plied Buss Creek, the river separating Reydon from Southwold, which had an outlet to the sea. A quay was built on the river Blyth in the mid 18th century and was a centre for trade including the import of coal, and the export of timber. Wolsey Bridge, to the west of the parish, is said to have been erected by order of Cardinal Wolsey when he was in Blythburgh, no doubt drumming up funds for his various educational projects (see Ipswich). It carried cattle to Ipswich market across the marshland, and is now a causeway.

The late 17th century Reydon Hall (1682 is the date given on one of the Dutch gables) stands next to the mainly 14th century church of St Margaret, which was the mother church to Southwold. The hall was altered considerably in 1860, and had the Strickland family among its occupants. (The current owners are related to friends of mine, and I had the chance to have a look inside. It is vast!) Agnes Strickland, famed for her historical writings, in particular *Lives of the Queens of England*, which she wrote in conjunction with her sister, was born here in 1796. She ended her days in Southwold.

Australians are still divided on the question of monarchy. The

Earl of Stradbroke, known affectionately as the 'Aussie Earl', was a sheep farmer in Australia before inheriting nearby Henham House, and his title, in the 1980s. Henham is the seat of the family of Rous, who have lived here since the 16th century, subsequently acquiring the title of Earl of Stradbroke; the village from which the family originated. The original Elizabethan mansion was gutted by fire in 1773 when the owner was away. It seemed his butler got a bit squiffy, knocked over a candle and only the frame of the hall was still standing the next day. Oops! A neo-classical structure from the early 19th century was pulled down in 1953 and only the stables and dovecote remain along with a crinkle-crankle wall in the gardens. Humphry Repton got his hands on the surrounding parkland and several of his original oaks remain.

ROUGHAM

—— 'It is a wise man who knows when he is happy. I had known nothing but happiness in Suffolk ... the English landscape at its subtlest and best'. And who would dare to contradict American airman John T. Appleby, who penned these immortal words while stationed at the old airfield to the north during the Second World War. (Royalties from his book *Suffolk Summer* go towards maintaining a memorial rose garden in Bury's Abbey Gardens.)

Can little have really changed in the 50 plus years that have passed? Rougham still has a serene air. The fine old timber-framed buildings and thatched roofs; the splendid 14th century flint church with its old chimneys, lovely wooden lychgate and weathered sundial. It is in superb condition and unlike Edmundsbury, finished! Wonderful topiary towers stand high above neat headstones. There is a memorial to Sir Jeffrey Burwell, grandfather of 'first Prime Minister', Sir Robert Walpole. Head through the field opposite St Mary's and look back at the church through the avenue of veteran limes, and the view is timeless. Fields of rape form an edge around the village like fields of dreams.

Rather more has, I suspect, changed since the Romans were here. To the south, the Ixworth to Long Melford Roman road intersects the Rougham Green road at Eastlow Hill where a Roman barrow, the largest of a group of four, was excavated in the 1840s. Remains of a second can be found in Link Wood near Little Welnetham. Other Roman constructions have been found

Rougham church seen from Lime Avenue.

nearby. New buildings spring up occasionally in Rougham but they don't encroach. Fortunately this tends to be the case in Suffolk. No one has the heart to destroy the character of these lovely communities. Mr Appleby from Arkansas would be happy about this.

He would surely also be pleased that a memorial is planned at Moreton Hall community centre near Bury for the five crew who died on 6th January 1945 when their Mission Mistress B17 Flying Fortress crashed on take off from Rougham airfield. A pile of metal scraps and a machine gun case were found in 1994 hidden in a woodland area nearby.

SANTON DOWNHAM

—— The soils in Suffolk have given rise to three main landscapes: The Sandlings, High Suffolk and Breckland. This remote village in Breckland, on the edge of the county in the Thetford Forest, close to the river Little Ouse, has been largely turned over to what has become the most extensive lowland pine forest in the UK. Santon was built on the shifting Breckland sands, and in the 17th century was as good as buried, Pompeii style.

The year was 1668, forever etched on the memory of local people as the year of the great sand floods. South-west winds blew the soil from Lakenheath warren, covering the village with great waves of sand dunes. Only Lawrence of Arabia would have felt at home. A number were killed and many houses were ruined, but High Lodge House survived. Many believe these shifting sands probably accounted more for the depopulation of Breckland villages than the Plague. Measures were taken to control the problem, including planting furze hedges, but it was many years before the sands settled. Later the hardy Scots pine was planted, and in 1922 the Forestry Commission began a massive afforestation scheme, planting in the first instance a mixture of deciduous and evergreen trees, and finally a concentration of conifers.

The church of St Mary has a Perpendicular west tower with the names of those who helped to pay for its erection in the 15th century carved into the stone at its foot, including references to John and Margaret Reve, members of a family who grappled with the sand-flood. The Suffolk Naturalists' Trust now leases Wangford Warren where the sand dunes are graphic examples of the wind-action that nearly destroyed Santon Downham.

SAXMUNDHAM

—— Although lagging behind near neighbours Aldeburgh and Framlingham in the fashion stakes, the town is not without its supporters, and during the weekly market, Market Place positively bustles. King Edward II granted the original market to Thomas de Verlay, lord of the manor, in 1310. Market day was changed from Thursdays to Wednesdays in 1854, but otherwise continuity is the name of the game in this sleepy market town.

The Long family presented Market Hall, in the High Street, to the town in 1864. Charles Long, MP for Dunwich in 1714, was the first member of the family to settle here. Although he was not Suffolk-born, he as good as bought his way into the landed gentry after inheriting a considerable slice of plantation land in Jamaica.

Hurts Hall, the neo-Elizabethan pile on the road to Sternfield, was built by the Longs in 1893 and was to be their home until the 1950s. The flint church of St John the Baptist, now illuminated to great effect, which stands on the estate boundary to the north of the hall, was the setting for the wedding of Saxmundham's famous son Henry Bright (1810-73), the landscape painter who worked extensively in coloured-chalk as well as oil and watercolour, and as a child lived at Park (now Brook) Cottage, on the Kelsale road.

He and his wife moved to London where Bright hit the big time after he exhibited his paintings at the Royal Academy in 1843. He taught several members of the aristocracy, and his work caught the eye of Queen Victoria, who bought one of his paintings. However, he never lost touch with his home town and moved back in 1858. When the house was sold in 1871, some of his pictures fetched the princely sum of £4 10s. I've been trying to get hold of a Bright painting ever since I started researching him. It ain't easy.

SHELLEY

────── There had always been suspicions that the moated garden of the mainly Tudor Shelley Hall might not be all that it appeared to be. Some thought hidden underneath was a medieval garden belonging to a house from the same period. There might be a dovecote too. The producers of the *Lost Garden* television series decided to investigate; an excuse for filming in the delightful western slope of the Brett valley perhaps? The surrounding peaceful meadows were about to be invaded like never before.

So does the hall stand beside the moat of its predecessor? A check with Suffolk County Record Office confirmed a date of 1519 when the garden was first created. The same time that Sir Philip Tylney (Tilney), a courtier, built the house. He entertained Elizabeth I here. One of his descendants was later involved with a group of Catholic plotters, led by Sir Antony Babington (the 'Plot of Ballentyne') to free her cousin Mary Queen of Scots from her imprisonment, install her as monarch and assassinate Elizabeth. As we all know, it didn't work. Tylney was convicted and hung, drawn and quartered in 1586, just a day short of his 25th birthday.

To show his wealth, Sir Philip built a church 100 yards from the hall, which, as was common with a lot of great halls, became effectively a chapel for the house. It has been restored over the centuries and the Tylney Chapel is now the vestry north of the chancel. The church is on the right inside the gates of the hall, past the old lodge which has buttresses reminiscent of Cressingham Priory in Norfolk, some say.

The television crew worked on trying to recreate the garden as it might have been. Finding some of the appropriate flowers proved a challenge. As Mrs Tessa Scott, the hall's owner told me, the choice of climbing roses, for example, is not as good now as it was then. She has plans to plant honeysuckle, lilies and vines, and will be hosting garden walkabouts on certain days in the summer in aid of the church.

SHIPMEADOW

In Georgian times poverty was a major problem in Suffolk, so each of the 94 parishes had its own workhouse where the poor of a Hundred (20 to 30 parishes) would gather in one building. The one at Shipmeadow was built between 1765 and 1767, named the Wangford Union Workhouse, and remained here until 1938. 'A prison with a milder name, which few inhabit without dread or shame', in the view of the poet George Crabbe.

The original building can be seen on the Bungay-Beccles road, with wonderful views of the Waveney to the north. The diary of an inmate, extracts of which are held at Lowestoft records office, makes entertaining reading and illustrates how a mild transgression from the straight and narrow could see you bound within the workhouse walls. A schoolteacher in Bungay who apparently had hit the bottle rather too frequently, entered the workhouse in 1837 and apart from a few days out, stayed until 1850.

His entry for 22nd June 1843, reads: 'This morning about 5 o'clock an alarm of fire was raised ... a young woman named Watson drew on a pair of Mr Riches' boots and with no other protection from the cold, except a petticoat and a night gown, entered the pond and filled pails of water for the men – an act of female heroism that was very honourable. She posses(ses) a robust constitution and is rather good looking in person – in character, as respects chastity, etc, etc NIL. Frailty, thy name is WOMAN'. The workhouse eventually became a poultry farm, with turkeys roosting among the cast iron bedsteads, before being sold.

Women who left the straight and narrow paid penance in the Shipmeadow Penitentiary for Fallen Women which opened in 1854 on the site of Nunnery Farm, opposite an hotel. The 'penitents' wore lilac gowns and white caps and carried out their chores in silence. The centre was moved to Ditchingham when its marshland position became something of a health risk.

SIBTON

You might be happy to know that the quality of the air you are breathing here is being watched. The national ozone monitoring station is at the highest point of the village. Sibton's ozone levels are now renowned, apparently. I'm not sure whether for good or bad!

On a rather lower level, and before you get to Sibton proper, take a little diversion at the Sibton Green turning and you instantly enter a vast parkland area. There are a number of 'private' signs dotted around but as it is hard to distinguish where private land begins and public footpaths end, it is an enchanting adventure. Past Sibton Park House, winding around an ivy-clad cottage where Dickens' Miss Havisham could almost be still brooding about her non-wedding day. Then onto a long brick wall (hiding what?) arriving at the clockhouse where the hands have stopped at half past two. I went in the early spring when crocuses were sprouting around the numerous ponds, which are indicative of the large community living here centuries ago when Sibton was larger than Peasenhall. Each small-holder would dig a pond to provide water to sustain his family, pigs and sheep.

At Domesday Sibton was called 'Sibbetuna', meaning 'Sibba's Homestead'. At that time Robert Malet held the manor and the church of St Peter had already been erected. In 1149 the only Cistercian abbey in Suffolk, with an abbot and twelve monks, was founded here by Malet's nephew, Sir William de Cheney. This was a very active and prosperous community and the list of benefactors to the abbey is one of the longest in East Anglia. The ruins of the Norman arcade stand isolated among the grasses of the watermeadows. Disciples of St Bernard made a point of setting up their foundations in remote countryside. The ruins are usually hidden in summer, but when the church has a fete, a local farmer often gives rides on his tractor for a closer look.

St Peter's is a good starting point for one of the circular footpaths around the village. As the helpful parish path leaflet delights in informing visitors, if you have a hankering for going around Cape Horn and taking in Hyde Park along the way, this is your big chance.

The discovery in 1862 by Aldeburgh historian Septimus Davidson of a 48 foot clinker-built Saxon burial ship under the bracken of Church Common, could be the outline of a plot by one of Suffolk's numerous mystery writers. Does it date from the same period as Sutton Hoo? Who had plundered the grave, but left a gold ring untouched? The road from the church to Aldeburgh runs through the middle of the cemetery. Some of the cremation urns found can be seen at the Moot Hall, Aldeburgh. Who did they belong to?

Maybe Benjamin Britten could have written an opera about it. The founder of the Aldeburgh Festival lived at the Old Mill near the school in 1947 and wrote the opera, *Peter Grimes*, here. The first floor balcony has views out across spectacular scenery to the Maltings. These fine buildings were the work of Newson Garrett whose initials can be seen over the central archway along with the date, 1859, etched in bricks made at his own works.

Garrett bought the existing corn business, with its wharf and granaries, and then constructed the malt houses to his own design for malting barley. Vessels carrying a hundred tonnes of barley shipped from London would arrive at the quay and be stored in the warehouses on both sides of the bridge. Now it is a regular dock for old sailing barges and visiting yachtsmen. There would have been a Georgian hump bridge here then. It was demolished in 1959 but the bricks were saved and can be seen in the bus shelter, on the common, the top of which forms a hump.

Maybe barley makes you brainy. Of Garrett's six daughters, Elizabeth became the first woman in this country to qualify as a doctor, and founded the Elizabeth Garrett Anderson Hospital in London, before becoming the country's first woman mayor. Another daughter was a suffragette; a third an interior designer. Garrett went on to build various houses in Aldeburgh, as well as serving three terms as mayor, before Elizabeth. The Garretts were not noted for their singing, which is a shame as the acoustics of the Maltings Concert Hall, setting for the annual Aldeburgh Festival, are superb. The location isn't bad either, set in the reeds that line the mud flats of the Alde.

—— Home to the Old Minster; one of the most difficult places to find in the county, hidden away as it is among fields, but I will tell you how to find it!

The ruins lie in the grounds of the moated South Elmham Hall, which dates from the 16th century and was once a hunting lodge for the medieval bishops of Norwich who kept a deer park here for their sport. It is now a working farm and B&B, where the loo of one of the bedrooms contains the remains of 13th century wall paintings.

In the car park opposite the hall are leaflets offering a selection of circular walks, taking in the local wildlife and leading you, eventually, to the hollow in the fields where the Byronesque, ivy-clad, grey flint walled Minster stands. (Alternatively, you can take an accompanied walk with the owners of the hall and Minster, the Sanderson family, under Suffolk's 'Invitation to View' scheme.)

The Minster is supposed to have succeeded Dunwich as one of the chief strongholds of Christianity in Britain. Not a lot is known of its origins, although Mr Sanderson told me it is part of an 11th century church to commemorate a 7th century wooden minster on the same site. (There is a view it could have been a cathedral, or one of Herbert de Lozinga's fortified enclosures.) The Minster is surrounded by groves of hornbeams, which give the effect,

South Elmham Minster ruins.

from a little way off, of the ruins being in the heart of a wood, and there are vague outlines of the tower which stood at one end of this single storey building. 'I often come here in the early summer evenings when a faint mist hangs over the ruins, or in winter when there is a dusting of snow. Then it is almost Tolkienesque,' enthused Mr Sanderson.

Possibly the most direct route to the hall is via the A12/A144 to Halesworth, through Bungay in the direction of Wissett. Then through Rumburgh. After St Margaret's church, follow the signs to St James' and the St Cross Farm Walks.

SOUTHWOLD

—— Artists seem to like this place. In the 1930s, George Orwell (Eric Blair), the celebrated author of such classics as *1984*, spent time with his parents at Montague House in the High Street, and took his pen-name from the Suffolk river. Alice Strickland, of *The Lives of the Queens of England* fame (see Reydon) timidly offered fellow author George Borrow the twelve volumes, when they bumped into each other on the seafront. He wasn't impressed. 'For God's sake don't madam. I shouldn't know where to put them, or what to do with them,' he is reported to have said. Alice didn't repeat the offer.

But we have to look to the Germans for the most novel reason for liking Southwold. Apparently after a visit, a German journalist penned a whole page in one of the country's regional newspapers, gushing about the town's 150 engraved seats. In his opinion, they are: 'true to the spirit of this place where the value of a bygone age still endures – even beyond death'. The hardwood benches are ideal for resting, reflecting and savouring the views over the nine greens, and out to sea.

The Germans had some making up to do in this town. The six cannons on Gun Hill are eighteen-pounder culverins cast in Tudor times and given to the town in 1746. In the First World War, the Germans mistakenly thought these were part of a fortification, and bombed them; they were removed during the last war to avoid a repetition. The cannons bear the mark of the Tudor Rose and Crown and legend has it that the young Duke of Cumberland captured them from Bonnie Prince Charlie at the Battle of Culloden in 1746. It seems that after the victory at Culloden, the Duke was sailing back to London from Inverness when he stopped at Southwold. He was apparently given such a rousing reception by the townspeople that he presented the guns in gratitude.

From Southwold you can be rowed across the river Blyth to Walberswick in style in a sleek rowing boat holding around ten passengers. True you can walk the bailey bridge about half a mile down the river, but the ferry is cheap, quick, fun, and runs regularly between May and September.

SPROUGHTON

────── Residents are supposed to look good for their age. Maybe they live the good life, being only moments away from cosmopolitan Ipswich, yet in one of the area's beauty spots. Covering nearly 1,900 acres of land rich in meadows and woodland, the oldest part of Sproughton lies on the banks of the river Gipping and dates from the Middle Ages. The 18th century, four-storey, red-brick mill, patiently awaiting repair (like so many in the county) almost insists on quietness, with only the occasional stirrings permitted from bream, roach and pike in the large mill pond.

The bells of 13th century All Saints church break the silence occasionally. You can even hear the rush of the Gipping, although it's been a lot more peaceful since the 1930s when industrial barges stopped plying their way between here and Stowmarket. The heyday was towards the end of the 19th century; now the old tow path is a refuge from 21st century pressures.

The villagers marked the new millennium with a green. The site chosen was a meadow, near the mill, now being transformed into a recreation and conservation area. The theme of the green is going back to the future; one of 250 greens being set up across the UK as a 'breathing space' in the modern world. Over 1,000 trees, including willows, have been planted along with a bio-diversified hedge to encourage all kinds of wildlife.

But hopefully the 'Wild Man' won't feel the time is right to make a comeback. The Wild Man pub has been in the village for over a century, based on one dating from the 1500s. It apparently got its name from a blackguard who terrorised the village, and was caught at the exact spot. In the village sign, the last to be made by 'sign virtuoso' Harry Carter, the Wild Man is seen carrying off a young woman; artistic licence rather than fact, methinks.

STANTON

The Romans were definitely here. The Peddars' Way takes a turn at Stanton Clare and at Chair Farm, to the north-west, a Roman villa was discovered in 1933. Between the 13th and 14th centuries, Hervey de Stanton, who founded Michaelhouse, Cambridge and was Chancellor of the Exchequer to Edward II, was high chief. Stanton was also the birthplace, in 1713, of Edward Capell who spent 20 years interpreting the complete works of Shakespeare, which was presented to Trinity College on his death in 1781. I wonder which play he loathed the most by the end?

There used to be two parishes, All Saints and St John the Baptist, until they were united in the 18th century. The church of St John still holds a service once a year even if it has lost its roof. All Saints has two memorials to two successive rectors who clocked up a century between them, Rev George Bedwell from 1811 to 1865 and Rev Henry Dudding, 1865–1917. Longevity is the name of the game here; the 1751 post mill still produces stone ground flour.

A shipload of tobacco was the commodity traded during the Second World War by Americans in exchange for the lease on land near High Wood, where a number of our cousins from over the pond still live. If you want to experience a flavour of the Deep South, nearby Wyken Hall Garden is worth a visit. Glories include an unusual dog kennel built like a chapel, a distinctly southern-style verandah and a fine rose garden tended lovingly by American Lady Carlisle, and open most days.

A walk along the main street past Stanton's attractive 16th century houses leads to a footpath known as The Grundle which is a tiny tree-lined gorge, and lovely for walks. The fine 15th century oak timbers in Grundle's House were studied by Dr Olive Rackham (*Vernacular Architecture* Vol 3, 1972) who estimated that no fewer than 332 (and a half!) of these fine specimens were used in the construction.

STERNFIELD

Sternfield House played a significant role during the Second World War when Churchill, Eisenhower and artillery regiment officers congregated in the pretty 18th century house to discuss tactics for defending the coast. They would walk down to Smugglers' Lane, an inconspicuous mud track at the back of Sternfield House where the regiment's cannons were kept. The story goes that before the cannons were test fired, a man would ride around the village on his bike advising locals to open their windows so that the force wouldn't shatter the glass! Churchill stayed overnight at the house; Eisenhower would generally sleep over at Hurts Hall in Saxmundham, so that if there was a raid, both were not killed in one fell swoop.

After the war the house was sold to Sir Arthur Penn, Equerry to Queen Elizabeth who would often visit. His nephew Eric then moved in and rebuilt the house, reputedly spending the equivalent of £1m on the interior. Princess Margaret was also a frequent visitor, arriving by helicopter in the large grounds. She probably nipped inside St Mary Magdalene for Sunday service. The church actually has roses around the door; which is rather appropriate considering Margaret's middle name is Rose.

The church notice board gives details of the weather for Sternfield and Benhall, compiled by the owner of Sternfield Hall, in Sandy Lane (right at bus stop). Compiling a report on the likely effects of a glacier passing through might have tested his skills. The glacier moved through the site at the back of the hall during the Ice Age accompanied no doubt by biting winds and the odd woolly mammoth! Boulders, or water-worn quartz, pushed ahead by the glacier are evident in a few gardens here and in Snape.

STOKE-BY-CLARE

——— Keeping a low profile in the south-west corner of the county, it has an illustrious history centred on Stoke College School. The school's Queen Anne house incorporates part of a Norman Benedictine priory. The foundation, originally at Clare, was removed to Stoke, and in 1415 converted into a Collegiate church of which the last Dean before the Reformation was the reformer Matthew Parker. Parker became Archbishop of Canterbury and Chaplain to Henry VIII.

When he took up his appointment at the college, he made efforts to safeguard its future and began by making Queen Anne Boleyn its founder and patron. He had a dovecote built near the gate with the Queen's crest (still there) reproduced in the brickwork. Of course Anne didn't hang around too long, but long enough to make Parker a guardian of her daughter, Elizabeth, the future queen.

When Sir Hervey Elwes inherited the bankrupt college estate in 1706 his uncle, Lord Bristol, told him that he would either have to sell the estate or marry a rich widow. Elwes didn't do either and he and his heir, his nephew, did as little restoration as they could get away with including, apparently, mending broken windows with brown paper.

Which is a shame considering by the 17th century, the village looked rather as it does now with a number of fine thatched houses, and a splendid green. It wasn't always so. Until 1967 a railway track bisected the green, but once it was removed, the green was re-seeded and sprang back to its former glory of a century before.

There are marvellous views from Cain's Hill. Somewhere to do a little plane-spotting perhaps? Between the wars Lady Loch was a flying enthusiast and entertained the likes of Amy Johnson at the College. On one occasion she landed a plane on Stoke field. She later gave a talk to the local children on 'how to help an aviator to land'. Sounds like she didn't need it. R. Douglas Brown's book, *A Village Heritage* can tell you more.

STOKE-BY-NAYLAND

—— When you reach this jewel in the valley of the Stour, the timber-framed houses, some of which date back to the 14th century, promise much. The Guildhall, which at the end of its wool-trading life became a workhouse, is now three private houses.

In the 15th century, the Tendrings were in control, followed by Sir John Howard; both families lived in Tendring Hall, which was rebuilt in 1784 by Sir John Soane. The building was later demolished and all that survives is a fishing lodge. Sir John Howard came into possession of Framlingham Castle in 1476 and became the first Duke of Norfolk in 1483. He was killed fighting for Richard III at the Battle of Bosworth in 1485. Not before he completed the building of St Mary's with financial assistance from wealthy wool merchants.

The church stands on a prominent site and its 120 foot tower is said to be visible from Harwich on the Essex coast, and at certain times of the day, and in certain lights, has a red glow. Apparently John Constable loved to paint it which would have pleased

Martha Smith, better known as Constable's 'Aunt Patsy', who lived in Stoke-by-Nayland. She commissioned a number of Constable's works, including three altar paintings, two of which are in Suffolk, at Nayland and Brantham.

There are some splendid brasses and monuments to the Howard and Tendring families in the church, and to Lady Ann Windsor who founded the poorhouse and lived at Thorington Hall, a mile and a half east, and one of the largest of Suffolk's oak framed, gabled farmhouses. It was built around 1600 and extended c.1700. The house fell derelict in the 19th century and remained so until 1935 when it was rescued by Lionel Penrose, a doctor with an eye for the finer things in life, who bought it for around £700. The high, deep orange walls of the hall are unmissable as you drive past, marvelling at what it might now be worth in this county of spiralling property prices.

STONHAM ASPAL

—— Just a mile to the east of the A140, this village has managed to hold on to several picturesque thatched properties. Among the trees, the wooden top of the parish church, dedicated to St Mary the Virgin and St Lambert, stands aloft. This is a unique double dedication and only one other English church (at Burnaston in Yorkshire) is dedicated to the Evangelist Bishop of Maastricht, who was martyred, probably, in AD 705.

By the late 13th century, the community was in the hands of the de Aspel family from where the village gets its name. They lived at the moated Elizabethan Broughton Hall behind the church, and the monument of a knight in the north wall of the chancel of the church is thought to be of Robert de Aspal (c.1330) who was rector here at the time. The church received its wooden belfry, clad in cedar board, in 1742. It was the work of Theodore Ecclestone of Crowfield, a keen campanologist, who had the original five church bells melted down and recast as ten bells (the only ten bell peal in the county) with the addition of extra metal. As the existing stone tower couldn't house the bells, the new belfry was added. Only two bells remain.

Outside the church is a splendid monument to the Reverend Anthony Wingfield (d.1714) who reclines serenely on his sarcophagus leaning on one elbow, his gaze turned upwards. He died of smallpox, contracted from his fiancee who he refused to spurn. It is in a rather poor state. A lovely octogenarian called

June who holds the church key (her house is on the way to the hall) said she tries to keep the ivy under control but would really like members of the Wingfield family, who are thought to live in Dorset, to get to work restoring it to a status commensurate with the fine family name.

June used to live at the hall where her son now lives. In the grounds are the remains of the old Upson Hall. He lets her keep her caravans on the path near the moat where militia men would gather during the Napoleonic Wars. Pictures in the Eight Bells pub show a group of such soldiers ready for action.

STOWLANGTOFT

——— The village sign portrays Edward VII on a white horse, shooting in Stowlangtoft Park, with the gamekeeper, guns and pheasants. The King entertained his mistresses, the actress Lillie Langtry and the Honourable Alice Kepple, at Stowlangtoft Hall. His wife, the long-suffering Queen Alexandra from Denmark, apparently didn't mind her husband 'entertaining' titled ladies but took exception to the 'low-life actress', Lillie Langtry.

Lillie could have stayed out of sight in one of the single storey, redbrick mid-18th century almshouses, with four doors and four windows of three lights, and signalled when the coast was clear. The hall, though, is grander, completely rebuilt in 1859 from the 1625 original. In 1750, the Lord Mayor of London, Sir Thomas Rawlinson, lived here. Ownership eventually passed to the Maitland Wilsons. In 1946, Field Marshal Maitland Wilson was raised to the peerage and a decade later the late Field Marshal 'Jumbo' Wilson rested here when he wasn't seeing action in Libya. His remains lie at peace in the churchyard.

The handsome church stands on a steep former Roman site above the village. There are a number of magnificent carvings: the font has eight figures, the choir stalls have standing figures on the ends and birds and angels on the misericords. There are nine 15th century Flemish carved panels with details of the last days of Christ, which were apparently bought from a junk shop in Ixworth. The rebuilding of the church is attributed to Robert Davey of Ashfield, buried in the chancel in 1401, 'a servant to the Black Prince'. Edward III's eldest son earned the epithet because of the black armour he wore at Crecy in 1346 during the Hundred Years' War between England and France. French connections continue. The village, seven miles north-east of Bury, takes its name from the great Norman family Langetoft who were lords of the manor at the time of William the Conqueror.

STOWUPLAND

—— It is hard trying to maintain a separate identity when big, bad Stowmarket is encroaching all the time on this village, where the Gipping Valley Path Walk follows the former towpath all the way to Ipswich. The double-sided village sign shows all the usuals: the church, which has a beautifully ornate 16th century Flemish pulpit, village green and farming scenes. To this could be added, the post office, two pubs and someone who must rank as a collectors' collector.

Charles Bird, a retired RAF sergeant, with 25 years' service behind him, has filled his garden with 200 horseshoes, 49 pumps, gnomes, model rabbits, toy cars, old number plates from America and even deer heads. His garden is fit to burst and has made it onto the village postcard list. You can't miss his garden past the church on the right. As you can't park in front, it might be worth pulling into the petrol station forecourt and taking in the spectacle from there.

The large, grey, Georgian Stowupland Hall is on a bend as you come into the village. There have been strange goings on here in the past. Before the war, at 20:00 hours each evening, tapping could be heard in the dining room. What was going on? Could it have been explained by Charles Freeman's diary entry from September 1825, which read: 'My wife was put to bed at noon of a stillborn male child'. As such infants couldn't be buried in the churchyard, alternative sites had to be found. Was it in the house? During work carried out after the war the remains of a child were found behind a wall.

There are probably no skeletons in the cupboards of Columbine Hall built in the 16th century of flint with a timber-framed overhanging upper floor; by 1844 it was a moated farm house. The name was taken from the early owner and lord of the manor, Philip de Columbus. It later passed to the Duke of Monmouth and the Earl of Ashburton. Turn right before the petrol station and right again out of the village and you'll find it set back from the road. The best views are from the footpath at the back. The hall is also open selectively during the summer.

🌿 STRADBROKE

—— Now we're in the heart of the impressive countryside of North Suffolk, less than four miles from the Waveney Valley. An area of charming old timber-framed houses, gorgeous cottages and fine churches. The 100 foot tower of Stradbroke's grand parish church is a landmark, acting as a link between the five hidden greens (enclosed around 1814) making up this extensive parish: Battlesea, Pixey, Barley, Wootten and Reading. There is still a green next to the pub where the locals play bowls on the century-old turf. It is a treasured pastime, constantly under threat from developers.

From Deperhaugh Wood on Stradbroke's north-west border, to where the B1117 crosses its eastern boundary, is around four miles. The village's hub, where most live, is towards the west of the parish. Such a large parish can afford to lose people now and then. Between 1831 and 1843 some 200 paupers, who had been living in tenements around the greens, were helped to start a new life in America, and a better one despite the revival of a corn market in the village at the time. The parish reached its peak of 1,800 people in the 1850s.

James Chambers couldn't settle. He has been described as 'a poor wandering Suffolk poet'; but he preferred the title: 'The Itinerant Poetaster'. Born in 1748, he lived as a pedlar, albeit a literary one, using his gift of composing verses around people's names, and hawking these from door to door in exchange for food or money. He came back to die in 1827 and his grave near the church is easy to find – it has a harp on top. Bishop Robert Grosseteste, who was born here around 1168, had a more conventional approach to the arts. He grew up to be a great scholar and theologian, also a respected author and translator of books. He became Master of the Schools at Oxford.

Stradbroke has a good network of marked footpaths to explore, with several new bridges over ditches, making them easier to cross. One leads past Valley Farm, down to the 'beck' and up the other side to the magnificent Thorpe Hall. Guides are available from the church.

—— There have been enough occasions in the past when I have been stuck on the A12 near here in a queue caused by, what seemed, endless road repairs. Not the greatest introduction to this otherwise commendable village in the valley of the Stour, between Gun Hill and Stratford Hill. It was originally a Roman settlement, with the river crossing forming the ancient boundary between the Iceni and the Trinovantes tribes, and later the border of the Kingdom of East Anglia and Essex.

A certain painter from nearby East Bergholt used to stop by. The village has featured in many of Constable's pictures, including *Water Lane*, 1822, and *A Sluice on the Stour*, 1830–6. The house in *Water Lane* is believed to be Ravenys; you can find the white and brick building down a track to the right of the church. The sluice is still there although the mill, which was used for the production of macaroni, and later, linseed oil, has gone. The master artist also painted St Mary's church. It is now isolated on the opposite side of the A12 and dates from the 12th century, although it was rebuilt between 1876 and 1879 in flint by Henry Woodyer, the most prolific Victorian church builder in Surrey. (He obviously lost his way!) An unusual complete set of letters of the alphabet has been carved in the stone walls.

The village was a popular stopping-off point for travellers on the London road, which explains why there are three pubs here; as well as the stunning Le Tolbooth restaurant, which lies in a sort of no man's land between Suffolk and Essex. Stratford St Mary was also popular with the geese and turkey drovers, 'walking' their birds to market in London. The village sign features a monogram that makes up the name Maria (Mary), which was a popular form of county decoration during the Middle Ages.

The Priest's House, west of the church on the south side of the road, is pure Elizabethan timber-framed. Near to the bridge is the Corner House with a date of 1596 in the plasterwork. It stands alongside the Weaver's House, testament to when East Bergholt was a leading cloth town in the 15th century.

🍃 STUTTON

—— Not to be confused with Sutton, this is another village best seen by foot, rather than horsepower; unless of course you have a steed conveniently at hand. The earliest settlement was probably below the church, where the original six manors – Alton Hall, Argents, Crepping Hall, Crowe Hall, Stutton Hall and Stutton House – were clustered.

A path down the side of the church eventually leads to the Stour; the river was once the main cargo route to and from London. The large houses fronting the river still have traces of the docking areas used by the Thames barges, which took away hay and returned with horse manure, and many a highly contagious disease besides! I did the rather pleasant walk at high tide when the estuary was awash with geese. If you carry along the river path you arrive eventually at Stutton Ness and the Stutton Hall estate.

The church is a mile outside the present village; the original heartland was razed to the ground in an attempt to stop the spread of the Plague. Victims of the disease were buried in The Drift near St Peter's which has 17th century monuments of the Jermy family. Sir Edmund Jermy built the splendid Stutton Hall, with Early Tudor redbrick chimneys and pretty gatehouse, in 1553. The hall can be seen as you enter from Brantham, and footpaths lead close to the main door for a better view.

Crepping Hall, just to the east, has a Georgian front but a history going back to the 13th century. In the middle of the 19th, an attempt was made to bore for coal below the house. You can approach Crows Hall to the east via an avenue of oaks. Although Anglo-Saxon in origin, the hall has Tudor brickwork and the adjoining brick barn is thought to have been a courthouse. Over the past half century, a corner of the parish, including a watermill, has disappeared under the Alton Water reservoir (see Tattingstone). Susanna Boby of Alton Hall, which was also submerged in 1875, presented the brass lectern in the church.

SUDBOURNE

—— It is quite easy to forget Sudbourne exists as a real place. It is probably something to do with the fact that it is now a conservation area and slightly unfocused; as the gatehouse to the old hall, and the long, straight road running to the church, are almost poles apart, separated as they are by a five-way junction.

All Saints has an idyllic setting opposite Sudbourne Wood, where you can park the motor and walk through to the Baptist church beyond. By the 1870s, All Saints' church was in a sorry state, and the driving force behind its restoration was Sir Richard Wallace, who bought the Manor of Sudbourne in 1871 from his 'natural' father, the Marquis of Hertford. He was to inherit the collection of treasures in the Hertfords' London home, which is now better known as the Wallace Collection, in Manchester Square, London, where the *Laughing Cavalier* hangs.

Such masterpieces would not have been out of place on the walls of the late 18th century Sudbourne Hall, built by James Wyatt and restored by Sir Richard. The hall was pulled down in 1951, but the organ lives on in the church and the outbuildings have been converted into holiday homes. For an idea of what the hall might have been like in its prime as a sporting estate, and the backdrop, by all accounts, to some wonderful shooting house-parties, can I recommend Kenneth Clark's amusing tale, *Another Part of the Wood*. His book contains lovely old photographs and gives an insight into his slightly bizarre Edwardian childhood in the grand house and what must have seemed vast grounds to such a young lad.

At the junction of the B1078 and B1084 Sudbourne-Melton road is a wonderful, thatched, 'Hansel & Gretel' folly-like house; possibly a lodge to the hall. There were even children's playthings in the garden when I drove past. I clung on to what was left of my sense of reality.

 ## SUDBURY

────── Daniel Defoe described Sudbury as: 'very populous and very poor'. OK, on market day it does get busy but down by the Stour, the easy-on-the-eye scenery still holds charm. Like the wide watermeadows of The Commons, where traditional grazing rights have been held by local people since the Middle Ages, and which was part of the soothing landscape which inspired home-grown artist Gainsborough to abandon portraits for a while.

The Stour was the commercial life-blood of the town throughout the 18th century until the First World War, when horse-drawn barges hauled coal and goods up river to Sudbury, exchanging their cargo for cloth and silk on the way back. The large flat barges, known as Stour lighters, worked in pairs with the second acting as a rudder for the first.

The canal was 24 miles long and flowed through 15 locks and under 16 bridges. The locks were nearly all placed beside a mill, and strict rules applied to conserve water. Along the hauling path, two horses towed the barges upstream, and one downstream, moving at the heady pace of one mph. To speed up the whole process the horses were taught to jump on and off the barges, as immortalised in Constable's *Leaping Horse*.

Recently a team of house detectives set about compiling a Domesday-style survey of all the houses in the town to identify the properties of people like Samuel Courtauld, the founder of the well-known fabrics empire and the Courtauld Institute. He was an 18th century Huguenot refugee who opened his first mill in Pebmarsh and resided in Friar Street. The Baker's Oven in North Street is said to have 16th century timbers and a 14th century cellar. An ivory medieval chess piece came to light during work on the premises of what is now the Britannia Building Society. They probably know all the right moves now!

SUTTON

—— Part-time painter John Chadwick Lomax found his existing house rather too small. So he commissioned an Ipswich architect to build an 'impressive gentleman's residence' virtually made of solid oak throughout. No expense was spared on the stunning Edwardian Sutton Hoo House, the grounds of which were laid out to exploit the superb location on the river Deben. It was then sold to Colonel and Mrs Pretty, and it was she who organised the excavation of the mounds at Sutton Hoo in 1939 (which were to reveal the famous Saxon burial ship), apparently because her friend had seen ghostly figures circling the ancient burial mound. A local archaeologist set to work with the help of the Prettys' gardener and chauffeur.

The British Museum then took over the project pushing the local yokels aside. The Ipswich Museum took exception to this and tipped off the *East Anglian Daily Times*, in defiance of the British Museum who wanted the discovery kept secret. The Fleet Street hacks descended, commandeering every available boat from Woodbridge.

There is little to be seen of the Saxon burial ground, although plans are underway to build a visitor centre and reconstruct the site. The major treasures are at the British Museum, with replicas in the Ipswich Museum. The museum has considerable space devoted to the find with photographs, maps and models.

The parish registers of 1555 show that Thomas Wilson was the first vicar. He was the author of *The Art of Rhetoric*, a book first published in 1559 and still used in universities today. Later incumbent Francis Vidal was the scion of Jamaican planters; his wife's origins lie in another continent. Mary Theresa Vidal (1815-73) buried in the churchyard, has been called the first Australian female novelist. I'm sure her *Tales of the Bush*, among others, is a good bedtime read.

SYLEHAM

Having Hoxne only two miles to the east, Syleham would have to come up with something impressive to out do its neighbour in the history stakes. Perhaps it does.

Robert de Beaumont, Earl of Leicester, led a rebellion against King Henry II in 1173. Hugh de Bigod, Earl of Norfolk was sucked into the conspiracy, and no doubt he wished he hadn't been. A year later he was forced to surrender to Henry and hand over his castles at Framlingham and at Bungay, which was as good as destroyed. Henry employed hundreds of carpenters to prepare wooden 'battering rams' for his men to do the destruction job.

The capitulation took place at the village cross which once stood on the marsh land by the church, which is only accessible by a quarter mile causeway over the Waveney. The village probably takes its name from 'sylu' meaning a 'miry place'. And there is nowhere to get more of that sinking feeling than down by the marshy water meadows of the Waveney, where Jack-o-lanterns (known locally as Syleham Lamps), hazy marsh gases, would often lead people astray.

Saxon St Mary's has a south porch bearing the arms of the husband of Alice de la Pole, Duchess of Suffolk. Perhaps she built it? About half a mile to the south-west is Monk's Hall; a timber framed house with 16th century chimneys. Thetford Priory once owned the original estate and had its own church and mill.

The remains of a post mill, destroyed in the 1987 hurricane, cut a sad pose in the village. The mill was moved here from nearby Wingfield. A large watermill, long gone, once stood proudly above the river and was originally used for grinding corn. In the early 19th century it was converted into a linen factory producing drabbest cloth from locally grown flax.

TATTINGSTONE

Once upon a time (actually in 1764) a family by the name of White moved here from Gloucestershire and built a large redbrick house, surrounded by lovely gardens. They were very happy, but one thing was missing. They couldn't see the church from their house. So in 1790 they built their own version, the 'Tattingstone Wonder'.

It is in fact a row of cottages made to look like a church. From the side facing the house, the cottages have a flint front with church windows and flint tower, and the only give-away as to its real function is the chimney stack set in the middle of the 'church' roof. However, from the opposite side, the cottages are of red brick and you can see that the tower has only three walls.

The Alton Reservoir, on the road to Stutton, now separates Tattingstone Place and the 'Wonder'. If you live in south-east Suffolk the next glass of water you drink (it supplies something like 200,000 glasses of H_2O annually) might well have come from here. The reservoir is filled by water pumped along a pipeline from the river Gipping at Sproughton, four miles away. Before being flooded in the 1970s, the Tattingstone valley was a mixture of farmland and woodland with the stream feeding Holbrook Mill running through it. The flooding claimed a few historic buildings along the way, including the moated Tattingstone Hall. Alton Hall Mill was moved from the valley before it was submerged and can be seen at the Museum of East Anglian Life in Stowmarket.

Alton Water and environs now provide a haven for wildlife, such as tufted ducks and the odd great crested grebe, as well as somewhere to spot bar marigold, a water plant. You can also sail, fish and cycle here (bikes are on hire). Cars can be left at the car park on the edge of the village where you can then follow the marked routes around Tattingstone Place, or in the reservoir car park which, conveniently, is opposite the Wonder. Follow the water for around 100 yards and then look back for a view of the two buildings together. Perhaps it isn't as wonderful as when the Whites were in residence; but the sight of these two splendid buildings, separated by tall trees, reflected in the water, ain't bad.

THEBERTON

—— Charles Montagu Doughty, arguably the greatest of all Arabian travellers and author of *Travels in Arabia Deserta* lived at grey-brick Theberton Hall, on the road to Leiston. When he wasn't on his travels of course; he evidently found the pastoral charms of the county too confining for his restless spirit. His account of a trip to Mecca, as part of a caravanserai of pilgrims who set out from Damascus in 1876, is, I am reliably informed, one of the most absorbing travel books ever penned.

Colonel William Light, who fought in the Peninsular War with the Duke of Wellington, spent some time at the hall with the Doughty family. As Surveyor General he founded and planned the city of Adelaide, South Australia, calling one of the suburbs Thebarton.

St Peter's has a colourful Doughty Chapel and a list of rectors dating from 1305, including C. Ralph, MA, the father of my friend Orla who introduced me to Suffolk in the late 1970s. Mrs Ralph told me the story of a spy who lived at Theberton House during the Second World War. It is thought Mines Hagen used to go down to an old hut near the Hangman's Tree, on the way to Eastbridge, to give signals. During the Great War, a German Zeppelin was brought down in a field on Holly Tree Farm. Some of its crew were buried in the churchyard extension until the 1970s, when their remains were removed to a German cemetery in Staffordshire. The huge fire following the crash in June 1917 could be seen all over Suffolk, I hear.

A decade before, Arthur James Balfour was Prime Minister. He had a reputation for being 'decadent'. His niece Lady Eva Balfour used to live at Teapot Cottage. You couldn't miss her walking down the street, apparently. She always wore an eye patch, black beret and (shock horror) men's corduroy trousers. When she wasn't playing fashion victim, she took part in pioneering experiments in organic farming with 'soil as the basis of civilisation', at New Bells Farm, Haughley.

THELNETHAM

—— Hidden in the middle of nowhere is the only working windmill in Suffolk, lovingly restored by enthusiasts in 1987. The windmill owes its very survival to its relative isolation, managing to escape demolition after it stopped working in the

1920s. It is also the most northerly building before you leave the county for Norfolk, lying as it does half a mile east of Hopton church on the way to lower Norton.

The diary of a local carpenter records that it was built in 1819, in under six months, and modernised in 1832, the date on the cast iron windshaft. There are two pairs of millstones driven by the sails, and an extra engine-driven pair on the ground floor which was added later. Work began on its repair in 1979. 'It was in a terrible state, the sails were in tatters, the roof had gone and the floors had started to collapse,' says Peter Dolman, who bought the mill and with a group of like-minded volunteers, adopted it as the flagship project of the newly formed Suffolk Mills' Group. The huge patent sails can be seen turning most weekends, and the mill is open on Sundays during the summer. The organic flour produced here regularly wins awards. Peter is restoring Stanton postmill, near Bury, which stands in his garden. (Suffolk Mills' Group, Mill Farm, Upthorpe Road, Stanton, Tel: 01359 250622.)

Every Suffolk parish used to have a windmill; their turning sails were a staple of the rural scene. In the early 19th century over 500 were at work, mostly used for corn grinding, but from then on their numbers declined, particularly after 1900, in the face of competition from large steam powered flour mills. Now there are only 37 left, and of these only half retain their machinery. Suffolk watermills were much scarcer because of the lack of suitable rivers, but as they were larger than most windmills, over 50 have survived. The elegant white weatherboarded (latterly brick) mills with overhanging gabled hoist (lucam) and first floor loading doors, were often the centrepiece of a group of riverside buildings; the *piece de resistance* being the splendid mill house.

THORNHAM MAGNA & PARVA

—— It is gloriously wooded around here where fine cottages, probably estate buildings, line the village. Thornham Hall, or what was left of it, might have been demolished in the 1950s (was this to pre-empt the listed building legislation due to come into effect in the 1960s?) but the park in front of it has held onto its graceful oaks. Behind it is extensive woodland laid out for pheasant shooting. The owner has opened twelve miles of waymarked walks through these woods and along the meadows bordering the Dove. The old house was said to be haunted and, rumour has it, you might encounter the Lady in Pink near the Hennikers' incomplete railway station.

The original hall was Tudor and owned by the Killigrews who entertained Charles II here. It then fell into the hands of Sir John Major (see Great Bealings) in 1756, and then the Hennikers. At the beginning of the 19th century the estate was turned into an old French chateau with 25 acres of garden and melon groves. During the Second World War the army commandeered it and Italian POWs worked the land. Perhaps they should have planted olive trees?

Thornham Parva is an equally attractive village with an enchanting church, one of the few remaining thatched ones; even the tower is covered with a reed pyramid. St Mary's lies in a sheltered, remote spot and dates from Saxon times; the splendid splayed Saxon window in the west wall of the nave is typical of the pre-Norman period.

In the Middle Ages, church walls were often covered with wall paintings and inside St Mary's there are some good examples. These are thought to have been painted by an artist from a nearby monastery in the early 14th century. The impressive complete altar reredos, painted about 1300, was found in the attic of a farm in Stradbroke in 1927, and was rescued by the late Lord Henniker. Experts reckon it could have been made in the royal workshops as the design is close to that of the sedilia (priests' seats) in Westminster Abbey. In the churchyard are the simple graves of Sir Basil Spence of Coventry Cathedral fame, and his wife, Lady Spence. He would have appreciated the workmanship.

THORPENESS

—— Finding somewhere truly unique is always a challenge, yet this pretty holiday hamlet snuggling among the purple heather and golden gorse of the Suffolk wolds, fits the bill nicely. It is now enjoying a revival of interest which would please founder Glencairn Stuart Ogilvie, who ingeniously began transforming 6,000 acres of family estate into a model pleasure village among the dunes, in Edwardian times.

Thorpeness' trademark black and white clapboard and beamy houses in mock-Tudor style, still skirt the edge of the man-made fresh water boating lake which Ogilvie built as a children's adventure playground, with just a little help from his friend, author J.M. Barrie. Budding 'Swallows and Amazons' of the 21st century variety continue to sail around the tree-clad islands in search of 'Wendy's House' and 'Peter Pan's Property'.

Driving along the causeway from Aldeburgh, the House in the Clouds and the windmill pierce the skyline and give more than just a hint of the world you are about to be transported into; a world of which Walt Disney would have been proud. But in this case a living testament to Britain's answer to the great American entertainer; now nearly a century old.

Thought to be around 200 years old is part of the side of a large sea-going vessel, which made a dramatic appearance on the beach at Thorpeness, on the way to Sizewell. The timbers are about 40 feet long and 4 feet wide, double-planked and held together by a series of wooden pegs. Stuart Bacon, of Suffolk Underwater Studies Group in Orford, described the ancient timbers as one of the most exciting discoveries ever made along this stretch of coast between Aldeburgh and Dunwich. This shoreline was once known as the 'Bay of Wrecks' because so many ships sank here.

TRIMLEY ST MARTIN & ST MARY

—— Quarrelling siblings are nothing new. In these two distinctly separate parishes, although usually referred to as one, the most interesting feature is the position of the two churches. They are not in the same churchyard, as sometimes stated; though they are only separated by a few yards, and according to local legend two squabbling sisters built them. There is no evidence to support this fact though both churches date from the 1430s, and both suffered at the hands of Dowsing and his men, who expelled both rectors for their anti-Puritan views.

I am sure Sir Walter Raleigh would not have put up with any in-fighting. Grimston Hall was home of the Cavendish family for over 300 years. Thomas, the Elizabethan sea dog who accompanied Sir Walter to the 'New World' and was the second Englishman to circumnavigate the globe, was baptised at St Mary's on 15th September 1560. He set sail in 1586 with three ships, returning home two years later a hero of his time. It seems strange we haven't heard more of him.

In 1591 he set out again with five ships but the voyage turned out disastrously. Cavendish lost his life and only 15 of the original 76 crewmen returned. On the village sign at St Martin is a portrait of Thomas and the words: 'By God, said Thomas Cavendish, whatever fate befall I shall ever love dear Trimley and the oaks of Grimston Hall'.

A short stretch of sea wall is coming down on the river Orwell estuary in preparation for the creation of a new inter-tidal habitat for breeding and roosting birds at North Trimley Marsh. An area of salt marsh and mud flat will be created for the 20,000 wading birds expected to visit the Orwell Estuary during the winter. Salt marshes are virtually the only natural wilderness areas left in the UK.

TUNSTALL

—— Around a mile south-west is one of two lodges to old Rendlesham Hall. Ivy Lodge is one of the most memorable follies in Suffolk, according to Pevsner. The big archway has Norman-looking shafts with scalloped capitals and to its left is a low ruined turret also meant to look Norman. It was actually built in the 1820s as a gatekeeper's house for the Rendlesham Estate and remains a prominent landmark between Woodbridge and Snape.

Tunstall is six miles from the coast, but it is nearer than this to a narrow inlet used by small vessels and sea-going barges up to the beginning of the last century. The sea courses through the history of the village like blood through a vein. Barges used to carry the corn grown here down the estuary and on to London or Newcastle. Ships' timbers are built into many of the cottages. Smuggling was another lifeblood in the 18th century when such illegal goings-on were so rife they were almost respectable.

Near The Spong, a long strip of meadow surrounded by ditches, were two wattle and daub cottages, which locals remember were a hangout for smugglers on Sunday mornings when they would gather to drink. When a raid looked likely, they would hide their barrels of rum in ditches and customs men would poke around with a stick trying to find them. In the church graveyard is a memorial to Robert Debney (28) and William Cooper (18) who died on 22nd June 1778 while smuggling: 'Neither age nor sicknefs brought them to Clay; Death quickly took their Strength and Sense away'. St Michael's is rather grand, standing next to Tunstall Hall. I was told that the church was only added to in an attempt to keep up with other churches in nearby villages.

Tunstall certainly stands on its own when it comes to wonderful forests to explore. For some reason the word has not got around that this is a fabulous place for a constitutional. I often borrow Zoomer the collie from the Crown Inn, Snape (setting for the old manor courts in the early 19th century) and walks through the heather can transport you to Scotland.

UBBESTON

This is the territory of woods, spinneys and hills. On the day I stopped by there were also purple-grey skies ready to dump their heavy loads of rain on the lovely, Georgian, redbrick houses on the way to the church. Suffolk really does have some wonderful skyscapes at times!

The 17th century Ubbeston Hall was a tenanted farm of Helveningham Hall and generations of the Simpson family have lived here. They had been rectors of the church since 1857, and all came from the Canadian mission. One of them built the bridge at the point where Ubbeston and Helmingham meet.

St Peter's church, standing on high ground on a likely Roman site, is now the offices of a marketing company, but you can walk up the pathway at the side, to the back of the building, over flat headstones, including ones with skulls and crossbones; probably signifying the Black Death. The church has a particularly handsome brick tower with blue diaper-work. Former rector, Thomas Cowell, bequeathed 10 marks towards it in 1529. Nearby ancient Ubbeston Wood is predominantly hornbeam but there are areas of ash, hazel, and maple. You can find the thin-spiked wood sedge here.

At Ubbeston Green, just past the post office in fields on the left, is a folly, which doesn't seem to have any routes or footpaths leading to it. There one minute, gone the next, just peeping above the fields. No one could tell me what it was. But I was told there used to be a real green here, which is why all the houses by the post office are facing the wrong way; their front is where their back should be.

UFFORD

Uffa might not recognise his old stamping ground, but time has still been kind to this cute village which retains its core of old houses, insulated from the traffic by narrow lanes which lead to the fine church. The churchwardens put up a commendable passive resistance to William Dowsing and his gang of image-smashers. He spared most of St Mary's glorious wooden font cover (except for its statues) which reaches right up to the roof and has been described as the most beautiful in the world.

A large monument nearby is that of Sir Henry Wood of Loudham Hall, Treasurer of the Household of the Queen Dowager Henrietta. Dower House (the dower is the share of an estate given to the widow for life to make room for the heir in the grand house) is behind a wall, just down from the post office.

A sturdy horse grazing in a field opposite might have been a punch, if it hadn't been black and white. The area around Ufford is reputed to be the origin, in the 5th century, of the famous Suffolk Punch horses, the oldest recorded breed in the world. They are always chesnut (sic) in colour and generally a good 15 hands high, with a big forehead, deep neck, long shoulders and well-rounded rib. The breed was once considered ugly, and features such as large carcass and short legs earned the breed the

A Suffolk Punch.

name 'punch'. Catlin's Duke 296, born in 1846, could hold a pail of water in the hollow of his back. Suffolks are still bred at Hollesley Bay and yearlings can be seen frolicking in the fields next to Shingle Street.

Until the Second World War, this breed largely carried out agricultural work. They were also responsible for the bulk of road transport. They responded to calls of 'cuphey' for turning left, and 'woosh' for turning right. On Sundays, horsemen would ride out in their bowler hats, cord jacket and trousers, trimmed with steel-faced horseshoe buttons. A veritable fashion parade.

WALBERSWICK

—— Water and art have made a big impression. In 1450, thirteen barques were used to trade with Iceland and the Faroe Islands. Certainly Walberswick has a passing resemblance to a Norwegian village on the edge of a fjord, with wooden buildings and fishermen's huts lining the harbour. The fishing and shipbuilding industries brought a great deal of prosperity to the former town and some of that wealth, known as the 'town dole', was channelled into building the magnificent St Andrew's church, 130 feet long with a 90 foot tower.

Now to art. There have been estimates that a thousand artists, professional and amateur, have passed through over the years. It must have been something to do with the light. Wilson Steer spent several summers basking in the area's beauty, from 1884, and just before the First World War, Charles Rennie Mackintosh stayed as a guest of the director of Glasgow Art Academy, Newbury, who had a holiday home in the village. Mackintosh didn't enjoy his time here; because of his known links with Germany he was considered a spy and was banished in 1915. Others who have been inspired to pick up their palettes are Cornelius Varley and Peter de Wint whose early studies of Walberswick church are housed in Ipswich Borough Council's permanent collection.

A new wave of young artists began to arrive with the opening of the narrow gauge railway from Halesworth to Southwold, in 1879 (Walberswick Station opened in 1881), and between the wars, the riverbank was chock-a-block with artists' studios converted from the old fishermen's sheds.

John Doman Turner completed his masterpiece in 1931; a detailed, on the spot study of Walberswick, painted in watercolour and inks on a 123 foot roll of paper. He was essentially an amateur, which might account for why this is such a flight of fancy; where social history meets art with every brush stroke. The attention to detail is superb, such as the steam ferry tariff, and signs indicating that parking was a problem, even then. Richard Scott is custodian of the scroll and allows small groups into the village hall for a look. Contact him on: 01502 722577. Naturally, he paints a little too and is working on a compilation of the many artists who saw the light here from 1800 to 1960.

WALDRINGFIELD

—— Wander around this delightful village on the south bank of the Deben and you stumble across pits and hollows of all shapes and sizes. It is all to do with the once thriving coprolite industry, which operated alongside the river towards the end of the 19th century, after Edmund Edwards discovered the fossilised dung in a field behind the Maybush Inn; which at the time was the Cliff Inn.

Coprolite was dug from the fields and shipped by barge to the Fison mills at Barningham where it was ground and converted into super-phosphates or fertiliser. Records show that in 1843 as much as 100 tons was being dug daily. The men who worked the pits were known as 'The Red Men' because they would be covered in the coprolite, which had a red colour. Which is bad enough but, in 1872 when twelve kilns were built, the choking smog and noise must have been unbearable for the workers. The fumes were apparently so bad that all the windows had to be shut. Great if you are on the wrong side of the glass.

The industry finally collapsed in 1893 when the resource began to run low, and competition from other areas became too high. Men in grey then replaced the red men as the cement works moved in. And then it was the turn of men in oilskins.

The quay at Waldringfield is well known to East Coast sailors, professional and decidedly amateur alike. Cartoonist Carl Giles used to keep his yacht moored here, conveniently close to the Maybush. One of his *Sunday Express* cartoons of 1952 depicts the pub in the background of a chaotic regatta scene. Most of the time this stretch of the estuary looking over to Ham Woods is a haven of tranquillity.

WALPOLE

—— Throughout the 16th and early 17th centuries, royalty had a habit of changing its religious leanings, which in turn annoyed the populace, resulting in the formation throughout Suffolk of independent religious groups. Walpole Old Chapel, on the Halesworth road, is said to be the oldest surviving Nonconformist meeting place in the country (now in the care of Historic Chapels' Trust).

William Bridge, Independent pastor at Great Yarmouth, was in a sense the founding father of the dozen or so Independent congregations in Suffolk, such as Walpole. His congregation of Independents originally 'gathered' in 1649, meeting in local houses, and possibly the church.

Originally a 1607 farmhouse, the Old Chapel was converted 40 years later and enlarged and widened by a structure that mirrored the existing building. The interior is much as it would have looked in the 17th century with a three-tiered pulpit and simple wooden box-pews. Those who could afford to rent these boxes would have occupied the ground floor, while the less fortunate sat upstairs in the gallery; men to the south, women to the north. Servants, apprentices, children and others sat in the narrow gallery facing the pulpit.

The burial ground contains a number of mid 19th century headstones (now easier to see as the grass has been cut right back) including the graves of two ministers and several important 19th century chapel families. In the north corner of the chapel burial ground are the remains of a building, probably once used as stables for the horses of those who travelled some distance to chapel services.

Formally closed in 1970, the chapel has just undergone restoration, and not without incident. The gentleman supervising the work told me that they had unearthed a skull with signs of bullet wounds. They took it to the coroner who said he thought it over 100 years old, so no case to answer. It was carefully replaced.

WALSHAM-LE-WILLOWS

—— Splendid timber houses greet you as you enter. On one, the inscription reads: 'Our hoard is little but our hearts are great'. Which somewhat raises the expectations of this village which no doubt got its name from the weeping willows which line the meadows alongside the river Blackbourne, meandering through this conservation area. It doesn't disappoint.

The imposing Perpendicular church of St Mary has six bells, after which the nearby 16th century inn is named. Inside the church is a rare example of a 'crants' or maiden's wreath; a tragic reminder of an unhappy 17th century love affair when 20 year old Mary Boyce died from 'a fatal wound from Cupid's Shaft', as the nearby tablet explains. The 15th century priory, which stood here, belonged to the Abbey of Ixworth and is now the rectory. During building work, the skeleton of a young girl was found buried under the kitchen.

Ralph Margery, a local yeoman rose to the rank of captain in Cromwell's forces, prompting the Lord Protector to say of him: 'I would rather have a plain russet-coated captain that knows what he fights for and loves what he knows, than any gentleman'. Margery and his 11th Ironsides fought at Naseby, the turning point of the war, when although Charles' magnificently dressed troops put Cromwell's 'poor handful of despised men' to shame, the Royalists lost. Margery went on to fight in Scotland and the Channel Islands before his death in Walsham in 1653.

In the 14th century, Walsham-le-Willows thrived. Regular courts were held for the settling of disputes between the lords of the manors and their tenants. The court proceedings have been translated from Latin and published by Ray Lock. *The Court Rolls of Walsham Le Willows, 1303–50* gives an insight into life then, when fines were handed out liberally for such misdemeanours as leaving the oast door open. I wonder what the fine would be for knocking down a witch and failing to stop? The story goes that on New Year's Eve, anyone seeing a ghostly coach travelling the Walsham to Stanton road will be cursed. You have been warned.

WATTISFIELD

——— Geology and geography can work against you, or in the case of this pleasant village of cream-washed cottages, standing on a raised mound of fine clay some 16 feet thick, in your favour.

Thanks to this clay deposited by glacial sheets during the Ice Age, a pottery industry was well established by the time of the Roman invasion in the 1st century, with the oldest pits dating back as far as 600 BC. An Iron Age site was located on the edge of

Calke (should that be chalk?) Wood near Rickinghall Inferior and also at Peartree Farm, 500 yards south-east of the village by the source of the Grundle. Twenty five Roman kilns were also found on a clay belt on Foxledge Common.

With the extra skills and knowledge the Romans brought with them, the industry soon became the largest in East Anglia and continued flourishing through the Middle Ages. But nothing lasts forever, and with the firing up of the larger Midland potteries in the 18th and 19th centuries, the industry took a dive, eventually leading to the closure of the pottery works. The village then turned to agriculture for its future. In more recent years the Watson family, known locally as the 'Potting Watsons', continued the craft. Their first kiln dates from 1743. The signs in the village to Henry Watson's potteries would suggest all will be well again.

The terracotta arms of the De la Poles over the south porch could do with some re-working, although the fine chimneys outside the main timber frame of Wattisfield Hall look like they were baked to last in the 1590s.

During the English Civil War there were strong Royalist sympathies here which are remembered in the local pub; the Royal Oak. Its location on higher ground made the village an ideal spot for the forces of Charles I to garrison troops and organise defences against the New Model Army of Cromwell's Roundheads. Geography working to advantage again.

WENHASTON WITH MELLS

Maybe this village should be called Wenhaston with wells. Until 1955 when mains water was piped in, it relied entirely on water butts, streams and wells to keep it above water, as it were.

Water played a part in unearthing the splendid Doom oil painting at St Peter's church which was probably the masterpiece of two men in 1513, one influenced by the Dutch school. It stood originally over the chancel arch, and during the Protestant reign of Edward VI around 1549, appeared as a whitewashed partition. Its significance was only discovered when rain revealed traces of colour after it had been placed in the churchyard during church restoration work in 1892.

Around two miles west is the 16th century Wenhaston Grange with its Queen Anne front and late 15th century core. The Grange used to supply Sibton Abbey, founded in 1149, with dairy produce. Members of the eminent horticultural family the Tradescants, are thought to have lived here too. The village sign is decorated with foliage representing the plant Tradescantia. But Wenhaston was not the home of the first John who gave his name to this genus of plants that he introduced into England. As head gardener to Charles I, he planted a few in the gardens of the Stuart courts. Son John (he and his father were known in their time as 'the first English gardeners') wasn't born here either. It was Thomas Tradescant, the father of John the Elder who lived at the Grange in the mid 1500s. Confusing, or what!

WEST STOW

—— At the entrance is a stunning turreted red-bricked three-storey gatehouse; all that remains of a great hall, built here in 1520 by Sir John Crofts who bought the manor from the abbey at Bury St Edmunds shortly before the Dissolution of the Monasteries. The gatehouse, by the way, originally crossed a moat. Crofts became Master of the Horse to Henry VIII's sister Mary Tudor and her coat of arms can be seen above the gateway. She did actually stay here on occasions.

The river Lark runs through West Stow and was canalised in the early 18th century. On a sandy hillock beside the Lark, excavations by Stanley West between 1965 and 1972 uncovered evidence of timber postholes of around 70 small wooden, probably thatched, huts dating from the 5th to 7th centuries. These appeared to be used for storage and domestic industry, and for each group of around ten small huts, there was a larger hall probably used as the common room (the finds are on show at Bury's Moyse's Hall Museum).

If Anglo-Saxon man returned now he might think little has changed. In 1974, a five acre Anglo-Saxon Village Trust was established to create a unique reconstruction of the village. Drawing on the discoveries made during the investigations, one hall has been built along with five other huts with workshops. Using only the tools available to the Anglo-Saxons, different construction techniques are used to find out how the original buildings were constructed and what they would have looked like. The surrounding 125 acres has been made into a country park and nature reserve with woodland, heathland, river and

The reconstructed Anglo-Saxon village at West Stow.

lakeside walks. It is also the beginning of the two-mile King's Forest Nature Trail opened to commemorate the Silver Jubilee of King George V and Queen Mary. Maybe it should be renamed Mary Tudor's walk?

 ## WESTERFIELD

—— Now more of a commuter village serving nearby Ipswich, than the farming centre it once was, it still has a large area of open land leading down to the railway crossing (the railway was built in 1877 to connect with Felixstowe) where 10,000 troops gathered for review during the Napoleonic Wars. The threat of war and need to defend our coast once again bringing a dramatic, albeit temporary, increase in the population of many a tiny village. Now, as Dr Hyde, author of the definitive book on Westerfield put it: 'we've just about got the balance right between retired old fogies and the 9 to 5ers'.

Major J. Whiteford never made it to 'retired old fogy' status. Having survived the Napoleonic conflict, he was accidentally shot while out shooting. His memorial is inside the flint St Mary Magdalene church where a plaque registers the connection with

Henry Munro Cautley (1876–1959), famed for his standard work *Suffolk Churches and their Treasures*. He was once described as one of the few people who could 'restore without ruining'. He was also something of a sportsman and played water polo for the county. His gravestone is near one of the kissing gates. 'I often say hello when I'm mowing the grass,' said the good doctor.

The Swan pub used to be sited on the other side of the road. No one knows why it changed its position around 1845 when a local blacksmith and sometime 'beer dealer' operated it. It is now run by a lady who used to go to the village school which explains the pub's 'School Corner', where old photos of her alma mater are displayed. Around 1640 the Collett family held the manor, and in 1662 Bridget Collett left provision in her will for the education of villagers and for the purchase of cloaks, shoes and books. I wonder where those funds go now?

When it came to deciding what to include on the village sign, around twelve years ago, someone suggested depicting, shall we say, sexually liberated frogs. Apparently there are a lot of them around these parts, being liberal. The suggestion wasn't adopted.

WESTHORPE

—— Westhorpe's little known claim to fame is being the home of Mary Tudor after whom the ship, the *Mary Rose* was named. At the age of 17, in 1514, Mary married the ailing Louis XII of France, and was briefly Queen of France until his death soon after. She then secretly married her childhood love, Charles Brandon, Duke of Suffolk and lived until her death in Westhorpe Hall, then palatial and her favourite house. Despite this, she was always known as 'the frenche quene'.

There isn't much to see now of the original hall which was demolished in the 18th century. All that remains is the coat of arms placed on the new hall and the original Tudor brick bridge across the moat. The newer Georgian building is a retirement home. Where Mary is buried is not clear. She was interred in Bury St Edmunds Abbey, and after the Dissolution her remains were transferred to St Mary's church in Bury – but her heart is supposed to be buried in St Margaret's, Westhorpe. A modern board in the north aisle commemorates her, but apart from a rose in this aisle's west window, there is nothing specifically Tudor.

The church is mainly 14th century, though the tower and aisles were not completed until a century later by Lady Elizabeth de

Elmham, who was said to have been using money embezzled by her husband Sir William, one of Richard II's henchmen. There is a large 17th century font cover; its considerable size deterring 'witches' from abusing the baptismal water. Two local women were hanged in Bury in 1664 for sorcery.

There is nothing untoward now in this compact village, surrounded by farmland and with several houses of charm, such as the pretty thatched rectory, next to the church, dating from the 1500s. The village can also boast an oak tree with a keyhole in it, at Lodge Farm, as well as an ash tree that has square twigs. Now there's a thing. And for an example of medieval strip farming, a field off Ladywell Lane can enlighten. A tithe map of the parish shows the exact position of present ones, and where the other ancient strips used to be.

 ## WESTLETON

—— Most of the traffic through here is probably heading for Minsmere or Dunwich. Discovering this gem built around a village green, which slopes down to a duck pond bordered by a sturdy Suffolk mix of Tudor-gabled house (Moor House) and the weathered red bricked Crown Inn where Henry James stopped to sup ale, is a true bonus. Perhaps this is how the Norse invader Vestildhi fell upon it on his way between the old Roman settlements of Darsham and Dunwich; by chance.

Before a great storm blocked the Dunwich harbour with shingle, Westleton was a staging post on the road to the flourishing port. Many houses were fishermen's homes, and nearly every cottage had a small brick kiln in the garden in which herrings were cured over smoking oak chips. Quite a cottage industry at one time. When the shingle arrived, shipping went to other harbours nearby, but part of the market life of Dunwich came to Westleton. As the village prospered, the church came in for some attention and was largely finished before the Black Death came in 1349, and as good as killed the area commercially.

On the edge of the village, sandy tracks weave among the bracken where rabbits once ruled. Royal rabbit catcher June (sic) Perry, who died in 1858 at the age of 80, is buried in the churchyard. His tombstone reads: 'He was a Warrener in Windsor Great Park in the Reigns of our several Sovereigns George the Third, George the Fourth, William the Fourth and her present Majesty'. It must have been a solitary life, rather like that on the foreshore of Minsmere, where the remains of Ralph de Glanville's original abbey stand. It became a hermitage attached to Leiston Abbey in 1531 and one of the last abbots, John Green, became an anchorite with just the river and cornfields for company.

One of the great leisure pastimes here, the Barrel Fair, has become an annual event again since 1995. The original week long carnival started in the Festival of Britain year (1950), when burly men pushed wooden barrels down the street. Now there are races for both men and women using barrels made of metal; much lighter for pushing up and down the green.

WETHERINGSETT CUM BROCKFORD

────── I think we have all heard of Raleigh and Drake, the great Elizabethan seafarers, but what of Richard Hakluyt? The past rector of this parish is one of the unsung names of Elizabethan explorations. He apparently had his appetite whetted as a young lad when he spied the maps of foreign lands in his cousin's law chambers. Although he didn't travel abroad much, Richard's acquired knowlege of the New World gained credibility among society notables like Sir Philip Sidney and Sir Walter Raleigh.

When explorations to foreign lands were at their peak, Hakluyt drew on detailed accounts of these quests, becoming an essential consultant for new explorers. By now married to a relation of Thomas Cavendish the circumnavigator (see Trimley), the newly-appointed rector moved here (where exactly is unclear) to write his book, published in 1589 and amounting to over one million words, including some ripping yarns plundered from ships' logs. *The Principal Navigations, Voyages and Discoveries of the English Nation* was to become a must-read for explorers.

Hakluyt left the village in 1602 to become Archdeacon of Westminster, but he was in some ways still ingenuous. In 1604 he was moving in Gunpowder Plot circles without suspecting a thing, but he did petition the King for more colonial expansion so England could benefit from cheaper New World items like fur and timber. He died in 1616, and is buried in Westminster Abbey. Some of his manuscripts are in the Bodleian Library in Oxford and there is a Hakluyt Society at the British Museum, as well as a mountain named after him on an island north of Iceland.

The village sign features Hakluyt on the left and George Ellis, the unordained rector from 1883-1888. He was not a real parson and a special Act of Parliament (The Marriage Validation Act 1888) had to be passed to validate the marriages he had conducted. Winifred Smith MBE, postmistress for over 35 years, used to have to validate gun licences. She succeeded her mother and father in the role, and her house, with the post office in one of its rooms, has changed little since it opened for business in 1910. Winifred still gets her water from a pump in the kitchen. They don't make 'em like that any more!

WHERSTEAD

——— Power company HQs are not usually somewhere of great interest. Wherstead Park is the exception. The original plain grey hall was built between 1792 and 1794, for Sir Robert Harland. The old hall was seven bays wide and had a fine staircase. A canvas Canaletto, nine feet long and seven and a half feet high, graced the walls. Mrs Paul, who lived there in the 1930s, remembers the sweep of the stairs. She also recalls visiting old Mrs Dashwood who wore a red wig, was known as the 'Queen of Wherstead' and expected lesser mortals to curtsey in her presence.

The original part of the house looks down to the river and over to St Mary's church which stands on its own, away from the village centre, and has a lovely stained-glass porch. The lychgate (1894) is in memory of Foster Barham Zincke, vicar and historian, who lived in what is now the nursing home and would walk across fields of orchids to the church. St Mary's used to be a reference point when flagpole buoys were lined up in the river.

In 1819 Sir Robert Harland let the house to Lord Granville for £1,000 a year, and was visited by the likes of Canning, Huskisson and the Iron Duke, Wellington. In his book *Wherstead Territorial and Manorial*, Zincke writes: 'On one occasion when the Duke fired at a pheasant he hit Lord Granville in the face. The Duke said: "I have shot my friend, not my enemy".' The likely spot was Bobbit's Hole, where the sewage farm now stands.

The remains of the house are clear to see, standing rather incongruously among the new high-tech buildings. There is a visitors' car park at the HQ, from where you can then walk a very pleasant quarter of a mile down to the church skirting the edge of the parkland, and laid out by Humphry Repton. Sheep graze on the farmland, bunnies dart around in the small pine forest, but I sighted no pheasants. The view over rolling hills to the Orwell beyond is a delight. It is a shame that the bridge looms quite so large and the traffic noise is quite so intense, but if you switch off your hearing sense for a moment, you can just imagine how it might have been in the days of the gentlemen-politicians.

WINGFIELD

―――― As rural charm goes, Wingfield is up there among the best, lying so serenely in the Waveney valley it is difficult to believe it had such a political past. At one time, the village was home to two powerful and influential families who were within grasp of the English throne. The Wingfields were established here at the Norman Conquest and once had eight knights in the family, two of the Order of the Garter.

Sir John de Wingfield was a friend of the 'Black Prince' (Edward III's eldest son) and fought beside him during the Hundred Years' War. He was Chief of the Black Prince's Council and married his sister Elizabeth Plantagenet. Before his death in 1361 from the Black Death, he built the church and established a trust for a college for the education of priests, which remained so until 1534. The college was surrendered to Henry VIII in 1542.

Over the years alterations to the exterior of the building, including a Georgian stucco facade, have disguised its true age. Today it is the home of Wingfield Arts and Music and the original medieval great hall is the setting, along with other mixed period rooms, for exhibitions and permanent collections of ceramics and textiles. The college is opposite the fine De la Pole pub which is a clue to the second great family to live in Wingfield; the seriously wealthy and mighty de la Poles.

Michael de la Pole married Katherine Wingfield and built the castle, as the family seat, around 1384. The fully moated building has a twin-towered gatehouse rising 60 feet above the moat and is flanked by castellated curtain walls and corner towers. The timber-framed house is built at right angles to the gatehouse and is said to date from 1544. The castle is now a private home, and the main entrance is firmly closed. However, a walk on Wingfield common, which runs alongside the moat, will give you a good view of this architectural jewel.

⚘ WINSTON

——— Winston has been a thriving community for years; good communications could explain this. A Roman road runs on Winston's southern boundary while the river Deben runs on its northern perimeter. But it hasn't always been the most tolerant community.

In 1556, three years after the Catholic Queen Mary succeeded to the throne, Thomas Spicer, a 19-year-old labourer of the parish, was martyred for refusing to attend Mass. He had been arrested by order of Sir John Tyrrell of Gipping Hall and dragged from his bed at dawn by two fellow parishioners. After languishing in Eye dungeon, he was burned at the stake in Beccles. A moving account of his trial and death is found on the wall in the chancel.

Religious toleration improved when in 1819, a girls' school was founded by Dissenters (those not of the established church) in Winston. In the early 19th century, the glebe house was 'unfit for habitation'. Conveniently it burned down, and in 1843-4 the new vicarage was built – a Gothic gem, designed by S.S Teulon, and now The Grange.

The name Winston probably means 'place of wine'. At the Norman Conquest, Winston consisted of two manors, the major one belonging to the Abbot of St Etheldreda, while the other passed into the hands of Earl Hugh in 1086, and later to the nuns of Bruisyard. Latterly it was a centre of local wine making.

A full peal of Winston bells was rung to mark the death of Sir Winston Churchill in 1965. At the same time, muffled ringing took place at Churchill in Somerset.

⚘ WITHERSDALE & WISSETT

——— I was heading into Withersdale from Mendham when a rather long flint wall homed into view. At first I thought it was the remains of an old monastery. I decided to get out of the car and take a closer look, following the footpath along the side. A little door took me into the garden, which had been made into allotments. I consulted Pevsner to find it wasn't quite as old as I had imagined: 'Mendham Priory, early 19th century, five bays wide, doorway with four Roman Doric columns'.

Just opposite, in the grounds of a rather splendid Georgian house, is a narrow gauge railway complete with seats and signal boxes. A train enthusiast's fantasies realised.

Lying in a valley alongside the Beck, a tributary to the river Blyth, man has made his presence felt for thousands of years at Wissett. Neolithic flint tools have been found. The parish might well have been heavily wooded in Elizabethan times, if the number of farmhouses and barns built with massive oak beams are anything to go by.

Wissett Lodge was turned over for fruit farming during the last years of the Second World War. Around the time when members of the Bloomsbury Group, that closely knit set of writers, painters and intellectuals, left London for the peace of this gentle valley. Biographer Lytton Strachey was spotted. Perhaps he quaffed a glass or two of wine from the small vineyard at Valley Farm, to get the intellectual juices flowing.

WITNESHAM

── I asked at the village stores what there was to see and do here. 'Come in and go out,' was the reply. When pressed further the owner talked about the church, and the pubs. Certainly cartoonist Carl Giles liked it here and was quoted as saying: 'There is nothing I can complain about, or dislike, in Witnesham. Everyone is so friendly.' Maybe that sentence constitutes damning with faint praise, but after paying an initial visit in the late 1930s, Giles moved here after the war to farm pigs at Hillbrow, in the steep lanes behind the Barley Mow.

Giles claimed his country home gave him the inspiration to work. Friends such as comedian Eric Sykes and comedy writer Johnny Speight would often visit, joining Giles for a drink in one of the local pubs. The setting obviously suited him as 'The Family', including the formidable 'Grandma', emerged soon after. Paying the odd visit to Melton obviously helped too, as Grandma has been identified as a bit of a harridan who lived at Melton and who happened to lose her temper if things didn't go her way. Her father was a drinking companion of Giles.

Juby's Hill in Witnesham, was named after fellow farmer John Juby who obligingly kept a horse to help sometimes drunken travellers up the steep hill, charging them one shilling for the privilege. Rather easier to negotiate, but best done by foot, is Witnesham Hall. Park by the village hall and walk down to the ford to get a true idea of how substantial and stunning a property this is. It is part real Elizabethan (the three-storey porch) and part Victorian imitation.

It would be easy to get totally carried away about life afloat on this stretch of the Deben where the great Saxon burial ship lies just across the water in Sutton Hoo. You can never forget this is a tidal river where sailors for generations have set sail once upon a tide and where, rather less romantically, boats keel-over in the mud for half the day.

There has been a tidemill on this site for around 600 years; it is now the only working one of its kind in the country, powered from water released from a lock-gated tidal pond as the tide ebbs. The machinery is massive with an impressive 20 foot long and 2 foot square oak shaft.

The best view of the river is from the top of the mill. A vista that takes in the tightly packed town centre roofs of buildings like the Bridewell. The half-timbered house was used as a gaol to hold Dutch prisoners who had been captured in the fighting at the Battle of Sole Bay, fought off the Suffolk coast at Southwold in 1672.

Kyson Point, on the peninsula formed by the confluence of the river Deben and Martlesham Creek, can offer spectacular views of its own. It was from here in October 1622 that Thomas Warner from Parham, captain in James I's bodyguard, sailed for St Christopher (St Kitts) to grow tobacco and kick-start the British Empire. The first crop was destroyed by a hurricane but eventually it turned into a successful industry, along with sugar cane. *Wealth of Nations'* author Adam Smith acknowledged that the income from St Kitts' sugar was worth more than tobacco from the English colonies in the Americas. Warner is buried in St Kitts, with little acknowledgement for his efforts in the place of his birth.

Local artist Thomas Churchyard is finally getting the attention he deserves. Now regarded as one of this country's leading Victorian landscape artists, the best of his work is frequently confused with that of his mentor, John Constable. What Churchyard painted is easily recognisable, such as the Cherry Tree pub opposite what is now Notcutts, and the back of Gobbitt's house in the Thoroughfare. He was born at the Beeches in nearby Melton.

WOOLPIT

—— The white bricks, which used to be made here, were once so agonisingly fashionable, and equal in beauty to stone, that the Tsar of Russia asked for some to be sent to St Petersburg for his inspection. Ironically, most of the houses here are half-timbered or of old red brick.

The old claypits of Woolpit were originally called 'Wolf Pits' as they were apparently used to trap wolves. A brick making industry started here in the 1500s, turning into a thriving local business from around the 1850s until the 1930s.

Documents from the 14th century recount the legend of two children, a boy and a girl, found near the claypits in the 12th century. Apparently their hair was almost white and their skin green. The girl told of how she and her brother had come from a far off place called St Martin's Land and had one day walked into a tunnel, got lost and finally emerged at Woolpit. These 'Green Children' were taken to Sir Richard Culne, Lord of the Manor, who took care of them. So why green? Modern medicine suggests they were probably suffering from a disease like jaundice or gallstones, brought on by vitamin deficiency.

In the 1st century there was a Roman settlement at Woolpit, and by the Middle Ages the half-moated site of a possible chapel, known as 'Lady's Well', was a place of pilgrimage. The waters from the spring here were said to have healing properties and pilgrims on their way to Walsingham would bathe their eyes in the waters.

More recently there has been something rather unsavoury in the air. The famous 'Woolpit Whiff', apparently caused by industrial smells emanating from Rookery Farm near Bury, has been getting up the noses of villagers. Hopefully by the time you read this, the situation has been satisfactorily resolved.

WOOLVERSTONE

—— Viking King Wulf apparently sacrificed a local maiden on a monolithic stone here. Modern-day maidens make up the roll at the impressive Woolverstone Hall, now the permanent home of Ipswich High School for Girls.

At the turn of the last century, a Mrs Berners from the hall was driven over Bourne Bridge in her horse-drawn carriage. Apparently she had the bridge all to herself. Rather more traffic now uses the grand Orwell Bridge which replaced it nearly 20 years ago, and recently ornithologists have been hoping that by placing a small wooden nest box on one of the giant piers, peregrine falcons might be encouraged back to the county for the first time in over a century.

North of the hall by the jetty is the step-gabled Cat House; a Gothic cottage built in 1793. The north wall has a large three light window with a white cat painted on the sill. Traditionally a stuffed white cat was placed in a lighted window as a signal to smugglers that the coast was clear for them to land their contraband.

You can walk from the Pin Mill sailing clubhouse, past the 14th century church in the grounds of the hall, with stained-glass windows in memory of the Berners family. It eventually leads to Woolverstone House, built by the Edwardian architect Edwin Lutyens and the only example of his work in the county. Originally known as St Peter's Home, it was run by an order of nuns as a home for 'fallen women' and was latterly used as a boarding house for Woolverstone Hall School. It is now privately owned. I was lucky enough to have a look around a couple of years ago when it was being restored. The Lutyens Society would look on it favourably, I'm sure.

A footpath parallel to Orwell Bridge leads to Wherstead church, where Robert Gooding, 'a salt finer', is buried. There were salt works nearby and in the view of some the Orwell was once one of the finest salt rivers in the land.

WRENTHAM

—— This is a land of swills, crans and Lowestoft lights. Back in the 1940s, when the fishing industry was thriving, the fish were transferred to swills, around 32 inches long, and then measured in crans. A quarter cran held 250 herrings. So much willow was needed that rods had to be imported from South America. (Lowestoft 'lights' on the other hand were made of cane and were rather more flimsy herring receptacles, only expected to last a couple of weeks.) There is no trade for these baskets for the fishing industry today and swills tend to be used for flower arrangements rather than herrings, but signs of this skilled industry survive. Resident and former swill maker Frank Philpot makes over 300 different designs of baskets, hampers, eel traps and even umbrella holders for vintage Rolls Royces. I don't envy him the discomfort of sitting on a plank just three inches off the ground for hours. But at least the smell of fish has gone. 'When I was an apprentice the baskets were wet and stank of fish. No one would come near you for days!' I don't blame them.

Slate roofers in the 19th century used to sign their roof work with footprints in the molten lead. St Nicholas' church has just had its slated roof restored to protect its gem – the oldest stained glass representing St Nicholas anywhere in Europe, dating from 1240. Opposite the church is the circular village pound, built around 1800 to house stray cattle rounded up in the village. They remained impounded until their owners paid for their release.

One hundred and fifty years earlier (1637) Wrentham resident John Thurston rounded up a few disparate souls and set sail from Ipswich on the *Mary Anne* bound for the American Colonies. They originally settled in Salem and the Thurston family was among the founders of Wrentham, Massachusetts. In 1647 Francis Brewster of Pyes Hall, brother of the lord of the manor, was one of the original twelve to introduce Reverend John Phillip's new church, based on congregational worship, to New England.

YOXFORD

—— The Victorian nature-writer Clement Scott described Yoxford as: 'The Garden of Suffolk'. He probably had in mind Rookery Park with its Wellingtonias, the limes in Cockfield Hall, and Hyde Park. The garden feel continues with Mulberry Garden, opposite the church, the village garden.

The distinctive buildings lining the long high street draw admirers today. A wonderful mix of Tudor cottages of Suffolk pink (achieved by mixing pig's blood, earth, manure or similar with the plaster) and Georgian buildings including Milestone House, named after the 150 year old milestone outside.

In Yoxford's commercial heyday in the late 18th century, carriages on their way between London and Great Yarmouth would call at the old Three Tuns Hotel (now a restaurant), temporarily depositing their valuable cargo. Admiral, Lord Nelson took a reviving flagon of best Suffolk ale, and later, Charles Dickens stopped by for a beverage or two.

Chances are they bumped into members of the Blois family, successful London merchants, who liked to flaunt their wealth. They built grand Cockfield Hall which claims to be where Lady

Katherine, daughter of the Duke of Suffolk and sister of Lady Jane Grey (England's 'nine-day Queen'), was effectively imprisoned under orders from Elizabeth I. You can see Cockfield Hall from the A12, but for my money the best view is along the footpath next to the old gatehouse (alongside Horners) where once over the stream, this architectural delight of red brick, said to date from 1613, reveals itself among the trees.

Clarissa Ricketts, of Satis House, managed to take rather more control of her own destiny than poor Lady Katherine did. In 1887, she lost all her money at the gambling tables of Monte Carlo and on returning home, faked her own death. Sightings were made of her at Darsham Station, and abroad. Her old home is now a hotel. The intrigue would have surely appealed to Charles Dickens. In *Great Expectations*, a certain Miss Havisham lived at Satis House.

Cockfield Hall, Yoxford.